King Jammy's

To the late Tero Kaski who kept reggae alive in Finland

King Jammy's

Beth Lesser

Published by **ECW PRESS**
2120 Queen Street East, Suite 200, Toronto, Ontario,
Canada M4E 1E2

**NATIONAL LIBRARY OF CANADA
CATALOGUING IN PUBLICATION DATA**

Lesser, Beth, 1953–
King Jammy's
ISBN 1-55022-525-1
1. James, Lloyd. 2. Reggae musicians – Jamaica –
Biography. 3. Sound recording executives and
producers – Jamaica – Biography. 4. Reggae music –
Jamaica – History and criticism. I. Title.
ML429.J27L63 2002   781.646'092   C2002-901760-2

Interior and cover photographs: Beth Lesser
Author photograph on back flap: Katie Kingston
Acquisition Editor: Erin MacLeod
Editor: Micah Locilento
Design: Martina Keller, Intro
www.introwebsite.com
Production: Erin MacLeod

This book is set in Berthold City Bold and
Monotype Grotesque Bold

The publication of *King Jammy's* has been
generously supported by the Canada Council, the
Ontario Arts Council, and the Government of
Canada through the Book Industry Development
Program. Canada

DISTRIBUTION

Canada: Stewart House Publishing Inc.,
290 North Queen St. Ste. 210, Toronto,
Ontario M9C 5K4

United States: Independent Publishers Group,
814 North Franklin Street, Chicago, Illinois 60610

Europe: Turnaround Publisher Services,
Unit 3, Olympia Trading Estate, Coburg Road,
Wood Green, London N22 6T2

Australia and New Zealand: Wakefield Press,
17 Rundle Street (Box 2066), Kent Town,
South Australia 5071

PRINTED AND BOUND IN HONG KONG

ECW PRESS
ecwpress.com

Thanks to Dave Kingston, Steve Barrow,
Intro Design, ECW Press, and Micah Locilento.
Special thanks also to Ray Hurford and
Andrew Lee for their help with the updated list
of Jammy's productions.

I suppose it would also be in order to thank
King Jammy, Mama Iris, and the entire crew for
their hospitality during our many stays in
Kingston. I hope the book reflects how much
fun we had with them.

Featuring

·DENNIS BROWN·
·KA DEEMOS·   ·MICHAEL PROPHET·
         ·EDDIE FITZROY·
·KING KONG· ·JUNIOR DELGADO· ·JOHNNY OSBOURNE· ·ADMIRAL & · ·PINCHER·
    ·GREGORY ISAACS·   ·HALF PINT·
              ·BLACK UHURU· ·LEROY· ·JUNIOR REID· ·LEROY·
·LITTLE ·JOSIE WAILES· PETER METRO· ·SIS MAUREEN· SMART· ·ECHO MINOTT· ·Mr LE
  JOHN· ·SIS.JUNE·   ·ANTHONY MALVO· ·WOODY NOBLE· ·KING EVERALD· ·JUNIOR ?
PER BLACK· ·TULLOCH T ·JOHN WAYNE· ·DON ANGELO· ·L· STITCHIE· ·PRINCE· ·ECCLETO·
N PIDOO·   ·NATURAL VIBES· ·HUGO BARRINGTON· ·FRANKIE JUNIOR·
·? PROPHET· ·LITTLE TWITCH· ·MAJOR WORRIES· ·TRISTON PALMER· ·SUGAR MINOTT· ·FRANKIE WILMOUTH·
        ·MICHAEL PALMER·

**All the big names have
worked with Jammy**

Contents

Introduction

For nearly ten years, almost the entire decade of the eighties, my husband Dave and I travelled back and forth between Kingston, Jamaica, New York City, and our home in Toronto collecting reggae records for his radio show and material for our magazine, *Reggae Quarterly*.

We had become acquainted with a close friend of Augustus Pablo, Mico, whose wife lived in Canada, and he introduced us to Pablo and his inner circle of musicians. On our first trip to Jamaica, we spent our time at Pablo's Rockers store on Orange Street. It was here that what would eventually become *Reggae Quarterly* started up as a photocopied fanzine, first called *Live Good Today* (after the song by deejay Prince Jazzbo) and devoted to Augustus Pablo's flock of artists – people like Delroy Williams, Jah Bull, and Tetrack. Pablo, being a 'humble dread', often told us that we shouldn't devote so much time and space to him and that we should include other artists. At first we hesitated because we enjoyed Pablo's work so much and wanted to promote the artists he had developed, many of whom were unknown outside Jamaica. But as we began to explore Kingston musically in the early eighties we became aware of so much more that was going on.

A new kind of music was beginning to appear in the calm following the brutal election of 1980. It started with artists and producers like Sly and Robbie at Channel One, Junjo Lawes and his Volcano sound, and with a protégé of King Tubby's, 'Prince' Jammy, who was based in the musically rich Waterhouse area. As sound systems began to play out again in the relative safety of post-election Kingston, the 'dancehall' sound was starting to take shape, and young singers and deejays began to appear. Their ideas and styles were new and fresh. And they were changing the face of Jamaican music rapidly. We decided to start including some of these new artists in the magazine and we began covering the dancehall scene.

Whenever we visited Jamaica we were always impressed by the number of talented young artists, often as yet unrecorded, who were just beginning to gain some recognition in the dance. Yet these artists – and the whole dancehall phenomenon – were being ignored by the local and international media. Dancehall was considered a 'raggamuffin' music that didn't have the class or staying power to make it big. It was scorned as frivolous (i.e. not 'cultural'), and dismissed as a passing trend that would soon be forgotten. Time has proven both charges wrong.

The dancehall scene was where 'real' Jamaican music was happening, and it was live, spontaneous, energetic – with sound systems like Volcano, King Jammy, Metromedia, Stur-Gav (run by the legendary U-Roy), and Youth Promotion, and featuring artists like Yellowman, Half Pint, Cocoa Tea, Supercat, and many others who gained notoriety in the dance. Eventually, both Dave's radio show and the magazine became devoted to promoting these young artists and working to give exposure to singers and deejays who were, at the time, little known outside their local communities.

When Dave and I stayed in Kingston, we spent a lot of time in Jammy's yard on St. Lucia Road, Waterhouse; this place served as both his home and studio. A lot of great friendships were formed and we were able to watch part of reggae history unfolding. I interviewed people for the magazine and took photographs, while Dave found records and got dubplates cut for his show. We sat in on recording sessions and watched as Tenor Saw voiced 'Pumpkin Belly', King Jammy's second cut of the now legendary 'Sleng Teng' rhythm. We sat around while Mama Iris prepared snacks for the engineers and artists between sessions. We watched baby Jam II grow more and more like his father. We went with the crew to dances and saw the reaction as the 'Sleng Teng' rhythm was debuted. Everything seemed to be happening around Jammy's back then.

The inspiration for *King Jammy's* grew out of this experience. Ray Hurford of *Small Axe*, a U.K. reggae publication, had asked me to write something for him on King Jammy. But as the article evolved, it grew into a book and Ray told me to contact Tero Kaski, in Finland, to have it published. Tero, of Black Star, a company that put out the world's only Finnish language reggae fanzine (in addition to its involvement in other reggae ventures), liked the book and published it in 1989.

Unlike many books on reggae, *King Jammy's* makes no attempt to cover the broad history of the music or its roots in Jamaican folk culture. Instead, it takes a detailed look at one man – the legendary King Jammy – and offers a portrait of his times, a musically crucial period in the development of Jamaican music.

By focusing on King Jammy, I was also able to look at the roots of the dancehall phenomenon, as Jammy's story alone spanned several distinct time periods in the development of reggae. First learning his trade with King Tubby in the days when dub was evolving from the voiceless B-sides of 45s to the international art form it is today, he worked throughout the militant rockers period and on into the dancehall era. At the time we began to investigate dancehall, the international image of reggae seemed to have stagnated. Reggae, to most people outside Jamaica, meant ganja, Rastafari, and spiritualism. But the dancehall scene was different: the deejays and singers chanting 'under me fat thing' over the Casio keyboard 'Sleng Teng' rhythm couldn't have been farther from the serious, politically-charged, band-style music of Bob Marley. Not to say that dancehall music couldn't have a message: sometimes the lyrics were cultural, but sometimes they were downright silly. Musically, however, it was something new to the world. It was upbeat, lively, and thoroughly modern in its use of electronic drums and keyboards.

Today, we are so used to the sound of dancehall music that we hardly consider it 'foreign' music at all. We hear the influence of sound system deejays in rap and hip-hop; we see the hand of King Tubby – the late dubmaster – behind the re-mixed, electronic dance music so popular today; the very idea of 'rave' can be traced back to its roots in the Jamaican dancehall. Although people really did try to 'keep it down', dancehall music was just too wild, too alive to suppress.

Beth Lesser
Toronto, March 2002

The Tradition

The tradition of sound system owner/record producer is the very foundation of reggae music. The greats, Coxsone Dodd and Duke Reid, cemented the integrity of the relationship by creating some of the most inspired reggae ever made, initially for specials that were to be played during their own sound competitions. In fact, before reggae was ever put on 45 for sale, it was imprinted on dubplates especially recorded in local studios, under very secret conditions, to confuse and outmanoeuvre rival sound men. Only after much demand was expressed did sound men realise the potential for sale of these local pressings to the public at large. Thus, reggae music was born, literally in the dancehall, and kept alive by the dancehall patrons.

Jammy's has followed the tradition, and in the process has established the kind of musical empire comparable to Duke Reid in the '60s. When I first met the King, he was sitting on an upturned box in his yard with tools scattered around him. An air conditioner blade had come loose in the middle of a voicing session and it was creating too much noise to continue. So a time out was called for Jammy to fix the blade. Out in the hot afternoon sun, several artists loafing, smoking, his children playing, the clothes strung up on the line overhead, the tiny studio empty, he hardly looked like the legendary King (once Prince) Jammy who had been stringing up number one hits for so many years abroad.

The Headquarters

The little house at 38 St. Lucia Road has been Jammy's HQ since the late seventies. It lies behind a gate, all pink with yellow borders and neat white grillwork across all the windows. On the north side, a cement stairway leads up to the roof that commands a broad view of that mysterious and controversial hotbed of war and talent and crime and poverty called Waterhouse. And far beyond that can be seen the hills where only the very rich dwell in luxury, living in individually architectured mansions where the cool breezes blow and lush vegetation surrounds. You won't find the name Waterhouse on any map of Kingston, but you will see Olympic Way running north, spanning the eastern border. You'll find Four Mile down at the southern end, just below Tubby's place. Going north a bit, eastward is the notorious gully that divides Waterhouse from Washington Gardens above it. It's a small area really. The number 40 bus stops and turns around right in the middle, at the end of Bay Farm Road. From there you have to walk a little ways along West Bay Farm Road, passing a series of streets named after various Caribbean islands. You pass Trinidad and turn up the next, St. Lucia. At the very top, almost at Antigua Road, is the little house, once humbly hidden behind a hedge of green bushes, and now boldly proclaiming itself the house of Jammy, with every famous Waterhouse entertainer's name scrawled along the wall. If it's a dance night, the truck will be parked out front with an assortment of boxes slowly making their way outside to be hoisted in.

**Pompidou in
Waterhouse**

Pompidou
and Tullo T

The First Sound

Jammy grew up Lloyd James at 51 Balmagie Road, just around the bend from where the studio is today. As a youth he divided his time between school, courting Iris (who is now his wife), learning the intricacies of electronics, and playing football for the local team. He had quite a powerful kick and was a much-desired player. In a little room in his mother's house he began testing his electrical knowledge by building small amps and repairing equipment for people in the area. It was here that he started working on his first set. This first attempt was a modest affair meant for entertaining small gatherings, wedding receptions and the like.

Jammy ran it alone with the help of Franklin, who helped to wire the sound. In those days it was all vocals; there were no dub sides to records and no deejays yet. One of the first employees to join the team was a tiny eleven-year-old named Tupps, the selector who used to follow Jammy after school and watch him at work in his shop. Tupps was so small that they had to give him a crate to stand on to reach the turntable. But Tupps was dedicated to the music and to Jammy, and he wouldn't give up – not even when his mother used to curse Jammy for keeping him out late at night. It wasn't long before Jammy gained a reputation for his technical work, and requests started coming in from other sounds to build equipment for them. During that time he made the amps for most of the popular sounds of the day including El Toro, Lord Kelly, and Prince Patrick from August Town. Even Tubby acknowledged his abilities and he was soon helping out the King in his nearby Dromily Avenue studio. Tubby trusted him and would call him in whenever he had a job for him – if the amps broke down or needed fine-tuning. Jammy had a reputation for the neatness and care he put into his work. 'I used to admire the way he put in his register and the condenser,' Tupps recalls. 'He was very neat on that.'

Tubby was already going strong with his sound and had acquired U-Roy as the head deejay. Jammy too had to bring in a toaster and the first was a man named Carly who sounded as close to the teacher (U-Roy) as anyone could. Later, Lizzy came in to work the sound. Back then you could mash up the dance by playing selection like the Techniques' 'Travelling Man' (Tupps remembers that one used to 'rule dancehall'), the Paragons, and Upsetter tunes like 'Serious Joke'. Tupps' specialty was the Uniques' tune 'Come On Little Girl'. It was Tupps' job in those days, as selector, to run down to Duke Reid and cut dub at his studio. Thus, he encountered all the top musicians who were recording there, so he naturally favoured their music.

Often, as the sound grew, they used to travel out to Port Antonio and play a place called Mansion Hill. From there they would return to Kingston and spend the weekend playing Chocomo Lawn, Salt Lane, and Regents Street, before coming back home to play Waterhouse. They often clashed with reigning sound King Tubby at Reedie's Lawn on Antigua Road, next door to where Bongolegs the dread lived. The very first official clash the sound had was to be against Lord Kelly. It was a big dance and it was named the Candlelights and candles were lit and strung up all around the area. It was a ram session but Lord Kelly never showed up, giving Jammy the title by default. Thus, the name and popularity of this new Waterhouse contender began to grow.

From Canada to
Record Business

In the early seventies, Jammy took a few years away from Jamaica and went to Canada. As a reputable technician and engineer, he was in great demand for taking control of the soundboards at stage shows; he also helped out ex-Jamaican Jerry Brown in his Summer Sounds Studio in Malton. Back home, the Waterhouse set was left in the hands of Jammy's brother-in-law, but Jammy's relative had neither the interest in nor dedication of Jammy towards the music and it wasn't long before things began to go wrong. The set would break down, money was needed for records, and the crew began to get frustrated and lose interest. At that time, Jammy's brother, Trevor, phoned Jammy in Canada and recommended that he take the set off the road or suffer his name to go down. Instead, Jammy sent for all the equipment – the amps and the records – and started up again in Toronto where he soon became the ruling sound. It was when Jammy's baby mother Iris had to leave Canada that Jammy finally returned to Jamaica. During their stay abroad, they had had three children: the eldest, Sharon, and the two boys, John John and Christopher.

Back in Kingston, Jammy decided to move out of his parents' house. Iris, who had grown up at 38 St. Lucia Road with her parents, gave Jammy the little front room (her own room) to start setting up a studio, and she moved to another room in the house. He started out with a two-track machine perched on a couple of building blocks; all he had the capacity for was editing. A producer would go and voice some tunes and bring him the tape and he could run it off. Or someone could bring him the tracks of a completed LP on various tapes and he could transfer them onto one tape in the appropriate order.

Around this time, Phillip Smart, who had been Tubby's prime engineer, left to live in New York, so Jammy was given a chance to fill in and learn the ropes. It was in Tubby's studio that Jammy encountered two great influences on his development: one was producer Bunny Lee, the man responsible for all the hits, and the other was the eccentric singer/producer Yabby You who gave Jammy his first rhythm to work with on his own and encouraged him to start producing. That rhythm became 'Born Free' by Black Uhuru. Bunny Lee, likewise, encouraged Jammy to join him on a trip to England, where Lee could show him how the reggae business functioned abroad. With a few tunes of his own production – like that first song by Black Uhuru – Jammy and Bunny flew out. Back then (it was Christmas time at the end of 1977) the reggae industry wasn't organised and there weren't the type of big companies willing to release and distribute Jamaican product as there are today. So how did they find an outlet? Jammy recalls: 'We did it on our own. We drove all around, all about in England all over the country,' trying to sell the records. Jammy also had music with Cornell Campbell, the Travellers, and the original U.Black that he was trying to sell. Although the Black Uhuru song was taken by Fatman and released on a 45 in England, it never came out in Jamaica. Uhuru was a new name to people, so the tune never did very well.

In Jamaica, in the new year 1978, Jammy took the plunge and formed his own label, the original white-spotted one. The first release was Uhuru's 'Natural Mystic', a track that was also to appear on *Love Crisis*, their first LP. Jammy was attracted to the group because they had a new sound, a fresh sound that was hard-hitting, cultural, and progressive. With his knowledge of the reggae market abroad, he saw the international potential for a group of good singers with roots rhythms and dynamic lyrics. And he was right. By 1980 Uhuru was signed to Island Records and well on their way to becoming the largest reggae act in the world after Bob.

Meanwhile, Jammy was still working as a technician, building and repairing amps. One of the many sounds he worked on was a little known set named Tapetone from Payne Avenue. Since all the equipment was made by Jammy, Tapetone asked if they could carry his name in order to boost the sound up. They managed to reach an agreement and Tapetone assumed the name of Jammy's on the boxes, and people generally believed that it was Jammy's new sound. This way, the sound got a lot of invitations to compete and began winning title after title. Tupps was even selecting as the Jammy's crew had largely moved over to work the set. Tupps achieved a special coup when he convinced Nicodemus to leave Socialist Roots sound and come and deejay the 'Jammy's' sound. Those days, Barrington Levy was starting to kick up as the newest vocalist and Jammy's had a dub of the song 'Shaolin Temple'. These songs, along with Nicodemus' raspy toasting, brought the sound up to the top, where they were soon joined by artists like Errol Scorcher, Mama Liza, and Kojak. Just before the 1980 election, Tupps took off abroad for a time and Socialist Roots selector Danny Dread took over the controls. Naturally, the sound played a lot of Black Uhuru's heavy rhythms and they always got a response from Jammy's very special dub of the Fantells' 'Tell Me the Name of the Game'. Still, the sound wasn't officially Jammy's. It was Tapetone and it still had to play down by Payneland when not playing Waterhouse. When the owner for the sound began to show interest in regaining full control, Jammy gave it back to him without a hassle and decided to start all over again and build one for himself alone. That's when Jammy flew out to England again. This time he stayed longer and began building amps and sending them back to Jamaica.

Jammy mixing in his studio

From Editing to Mixing and Voicing

In England, Jammy met up with Mojo Records and started producing regularly for them. From there, he flew to New York and bought speakers, while, in Jamaica, his brother Trevor built the boxes for them. That's how he started out playing only locally, every Sunday night, in his yard for all the fans in the area. It became a regular thing to pop over to Jammy's yard after the Sunday night movies. The lawn was always rammed – with pure Waterhouse residents. The other crucial piece of business Jammy concluded over in England was to acquire a mixing board and a four-track machine for which he swapped Black Joy Records a dub LP. So 38 St. Lucia was looking more like a real studio at last. The dub cutting machine had been operating for some time already, and now Jammy could mix and voice in his own house. He started working with Waterhouse locals like Half Pint, Echo Minott, Junior Reid, and Pad Anthony.

Soon Jammy was off to England again where he secured a deal to supply Greensleeves Records with music. The dancehall hit-maker Junjo Lawes, the man whose music had transformed Greensleeves from a small, conservative record company into the hottest label going, had slowed down almost to a halt. He was spending more time in New York than in Jamaica and no time at all in the studio; Jammy appeared just in time to fill the vacuum. Greensleeves already knew Jammy and his music. Not only had they issued a Jammy's dub LP, but one of their first releases was the classic Junjo production *Scientist vs. Prince Jammy*, a dub featuring the rhythms from the popular Barrington Levy songs. Also, Greensleeves took songs like Johnny Osbourne's 'Rewind', Half Pint's 'One in a Million', Wayne Smith's 'Come Along', and Junior Reid's 'Boom Shaka Lack' – quite an impressive collection. They also released the Half Pint LP *One In A Million*, one of the nicest reggae LPs ever made. Thus Jammy assumed the role of new hit-maker and Half Pint became his rising star.

Half Pint

Half Pint with Myrie and Marshall in the streets of Waterhouse

In 1984 Half Pint was still working with Jammy in the studio and dreaming of creating his own touring band (to be called the Measurement Band) to take around the world after his success with the songs 'Winsome', 'Money Man Skank', and 'Pouchie Lou'. His agreement to soon start recording with Sly and Robbie excited him with the hopes of attracting an even bigger label. In fact, he did later join the rhythm twins on their international Taxi Tour and Taxi did release several discos like 'World Inflation', 'Night Life Lady', and 'Hold On'. The three also worked together on the George Phang sessions that produced the huge hit 'Greetings'. He never dreamed then that the Rolling Stones would want to cover his hit 'Winsome', or that the royalties would enable him to leave the ghetto and live up on the hills and come tearing down to Kingston each day on his brand new bike. Back then he was still a ghetto youth struggling to make ends meet in the fickle music profession.

Pint was born on Rose Lane, Western Kingston, one of seven children. He was schooled first at All Saint's Primary where he sang in the school choir. His secondary schooling was done up in Waterhouse at Penwood. He finished his education in 1976 and went straight into music – although it took a while to achieve any recognition. His teachers in school had always singled him out to sing at the Christmas concerts and the like, but the reggae scene was different: money was involved and many producers were reluctant to try a new singer out on the market. Still, Pint kept trying. The Jays were living in Waterhouse and offered to take him into the studio, but try as they might, they couldn't come up with the capital to invest in time, musicians, mixing, etc. So Pint had to wait. It was John Marshall who lived down the street who gave Pint his first chance. Marshall was working with Yabby You at the time and they were in the studio laying down rhythm tracks with the Gladiators. Marshall brought Pint to a rehearsal one day to see how Yabby You liked the lad. Yabby was impressed with Pint's rendition of Horace Andy's 'Greedy Girl' and took him under his wing. With Yabby's help in training his voice, and one of those rhythms from the Gladiators' sessions, Marshall and partner Myrie were able to release 'Sally', their first 45.

It happened that Myrie and Marshall were using Jammy's studio to mixdown the music and Jammy heard the new singer. Unlike other producers, Jammy knew the key to staying on top was always being able to come up with fresh new talent. He immediately took Pint into the studio and recorded 'Money Man Skank', a 45 that sold 3,000 copies in Jamaica alone within three weeks of its release. Dynamic, the distributor, was after more Half Pint music and even suggested to Jammy that an LP would be welcome. The *Money Man Skank* LP, with its unusual sleeve, is a classic. It only had five tracks but it sold like a disco. Greensleeves released *One in a Million* a year later containing 'Mr Landlord' and 'Pouchie Lou' from *Money Man Skank* plus eight others including the beautiful 'What More Can I Really Do', a perfect balance of love and reality. These two LPs from Half Pint truly helped to establish Jammy as a major force in the music.

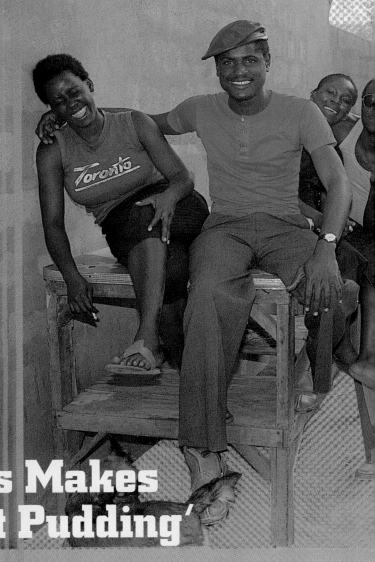

'Mama Iris Makes
the Nicest Pudding'

On any day in the yard one could see Pint along with Echo Minott, Papa Chris, General Leon, Junior Reid, Don Angelo, Tullo T, Pompidou and a host of other entertainers. Echo would drift in around one or two o'clock dressed in his finest after a late afternoon rise following his normal routine of bleeching the night before. It would take him a while to wander down to Waterhouse from his house up on Elma Crescent, across the gully, in Marveley. He and Leon would stick together the rest of the day. Pompidou, with his rockstone voice, was always to be seen with Tullo. Jammy's baby mother, Mama Iris, was always close at hand. Mama Iris stayed at the house with the children everyday, especially as their fifth child had recently been born (the forth boy, Trevico, had been born in New York). 'Jam II' (Jammy Recorder James) was their only Jamaican-born child and destined to be the pet of all who came by the studio. As tiny as he was then, he looked startlingly like his father and was quickly developing a similar demeanour – a childlike reflection of the big boss that charmed everyone.

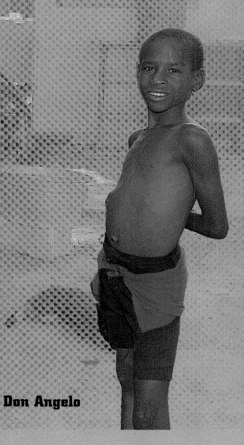

Don Angelo

Mama Iris in the yard
with Jam II

The kitchen of the house was stocked with **Red Stripe** beer, box drinks, and bun and cheese to sell the hungry masses of artists and sound men who were constantly marching through. The domestic attributes of Mama Iris have been immortalised in General Leon's 'Pudding Move' tribute: 'Mama Iris makes the nicest pudding'. The fact has since been confirmed by many – when it comes to baking and cooking, no one can touch Iris. But far from being just a housewife, Iris has long had the job of maintaining order while Jammy is on the road, of overseeing all the young artists who might be working there for the first time, of welcoming foreign guests and keeping things organised in a private home continually invaded by the public. The home itself has sheltered many artists who lived there while doing sessions; Screecha Nice, the idiosyncratic deejay from Toronto, lodged there periodically. Jammy's private life was almost public property – not an easy circumstance in which to bring up a large family. Indeed, all the washing was done in the yard where artists waited for the call to the studio. When washed, it was hung overhead on the line. A frantic dual industry was always keeping the place moving, the business and the domestic. When anyone had time to rest is unknown.

**Echo Minott
and Jam II**

The Big Clash

By 1985, Jammy's sound was back in shape. Stacks of boxes and amps had been carefully constructed in the yard and painted black with the orange and yellow logo. These were kept under a zinc roof at the back of the house to be carried out to the truck when required. But mostly Jammy had been playing at his own gates while building up to the official comeback clash – the clash to be held against Black Scorpio, the ruling sound of Drewsland, the strip just across the gully to the north. It was scheduled to take place on February 23 on Waltham Park Road.

Already the word was out and sounds from all over were coming to challenge the King. GT, a sound from New York that was temporarily based in Maverly, even came to beg Jammy a round in the dancehall, but GT wanted the locale to be Maverly Park and Jammy refused on the grounds that his innocent supporters would be killed trying to cross the gully at night to get there. The supporters make a sound king and Jammy had to look out for them. To cross the gully at night was, of course, the next best thing to suicide. Murderers and thieves of all cold-blooded types were known to lurk in its precincts awaiting their prey, to whom they would show no mercy.

In fact, nowhere in Waterhouse is particularly safe. The potential for violence is always there amongst the zinc shacks and tiny winding paths. The violence up by Jammy isn't political, it's purely economic (it's Tubby's area that flares up at election time with a border between opposing areas right down the road), but anything can happen at any time. It's unpredictable, unstable. Screecha Nice recalls being followed home from a dance one night when he was living at Jammy's house. Just as he was about to step inside, a man (who had been eyeing him at the dance earlier) suddenly jumped out at him, wearing a woman's dress! No one can call for a taxi to pick them up in Waterhouse after sundown; they may say they will come, but they never show. You may see a man come up to Jammy's wearing his jewelry in the bright afternoon, but when he returns at night, he has left it all behind.

In the opening days of February, Jammy's yard was busy. Bravo and the crew were hammering in the last nails and drilling holes for the final screws to complete the new equipment. All the time, little Jam II, not yet able to walk, was dancing about, getting underneath everyone's feet, and getting spoiled awfully for it. On February 16 a brand new, unheard-of-singer was inside the studio voicing his first cut. He was so fresh he couldn't get used to wearing the headphones and kept going right off key and staying there. As he sang his own nursery rhyme lyrics, he moved his hands and twisted his face into such contortions that the song became surreal. He meant, obviously, every word of it: 'How water walk go a pumpkin belly/Who tell me that but me old time granny/She say, "Saw, you must be going on like a ginal, woooaaa"/I said, "No grandma, I won't tell you now."'

Screecha Nice and Cocoa Tea smoking spliff

Jack Scorpio and General Trees at Black Scorpio HQ

It was the nineteen-year-old Tenor Saw, the kid who had once been considered the 'black sheep' of his family in Payneland. He was beginning his career in music and carrying a gospel flavour and a new singing style to dancehall. His 'Roll Call' for George Phang's Powerhouse label somehow got misplaced in the rush of 'Sleng Teng', but it stands up as well. When he did 'Ring the Alarm' for Techniques it rose to the top ten on both radio stations. His first LP, *Fever*, produced by Blue Mountain, achieved pre-sales orders of 2,500. That distinctive vocal style – flat, off key, nasal, but heavily spiritual – became the most imitated. It fit the current state of music, the drone of the new Casio keyboard creations. It certainly fit Jammy's new secret weapon – that 'Sleng Teng' rhythm he had just recorded and planned to unleash at the big showdown.

Over on Hedley Avenue in Drewsland, Jack Scorpio was also preparing. Scorpio, an absolute giant of a human being, started life as a *Gleaner* boy down on Maxfield selling daily newspapers in the street. With ambition alone, he rose to become racehorse owner, producer, sound system boss, and have a neat house with his own store in front stocked with soft drinks and snacks. Photos of his horses and trophies he's won adorn the walls. The sound is packed up in the shed in back, but it can be brought out and strung up at any time to play a dance, for Jack's yard is a two-tiered affair that also serves as a dance venue. Often on Sunday afternoons, going on towards evening, the sound is prepared for a crew workout. Selector Papa Screw pulls out the trunks with the specially built compartments to hold 45s, discos, and dubplates. Someone runs down the road to call General Trees from the house he just built for himself and his wife with its back to the gully. Culture Lee, an open, friendly youth, comes with Colour Chin, Lady G, and the rest. If Sassafras is in Jamaica, he will be found here too. Before Sassafras came to Scorpio, it was just a local affair, small time. Sassafras changed that. The sound started getting popular around 1982 with the new deejay and a pile of Don Carlos dub plates. It was Sassa who cemented the 'Horseman' tradition of the sound that came naturally from Jack's experience at the racetrack; Sassa too had worked there. When Trees joined them, his widely-known reputation for luck in gambling made him a true horseman as well.

**Black Scorpio –
General Trees
at the mike ina
horseman style**

Tenor Saw voicing
'Pumpkin Belly'

Jam II with $

Nitty Gritty

Jack had a few tricks up his sleeve for the clash and would listen to his music over and over on a little tape deck playing softly so no unauthorised personnel could hear. He laughed to himself as he heard the dub special by Bobby Melody that opens with the line 'Jammy get flat'. He was going to fight hard not to let Jammy come out on top.

The week before The Big Clash, the whole island seemed to come down with a very contagious flu, and the worst of it was, there was a shortage of Contact C. Sniffling natives were left having to make due with the locally made version – Puritan or nothing – though most who stayed with the alternative had the same result. Some desperately tried the old country remedies of over-proof rum and lime juice (sometimes mixed with coffee) taken before bed to make you sweat the bug out at night. In Jammy's studio, 'Sleng Teng' versions were being cut on dub, one after another. People laughed when they heard Tonto Irie's 'One a Penny Posse come ina this' as it referred to a posse of fancy bicycle riders from down in Early B's part of town.

The night of February 23, people began to gather on the Waltham early. The sounds were warming up with the apprentices while the big artists were arriving. Black Scorpio opened the showdown with the full compliment of Sassafras and Trees and regulars Shukahine, Culture Lee, Wayne Palmer, and Michael Jahsone. Jah Screw, the selector, was armed with dubplates by Frankie Paul (the Scorpio productions) like 'The Closer I Get to You', as well as Earl Sixteen's 'Sweet Soul Rockin', and 'Making Tracks', Bobby Melody, Little John, and Johnny Osbourne. On Jammy's side were John Wayne, Echo Minott, General Leon, Screecha Nice, Tullo T, Junior Reid, Tonto Irie, and Pompidou. Tupps was selecting with confidence knowing that he had a bag full of 'Sleng Teng' to thrown down. Every name entertainer was there from U-Roy to Leroy Smart to witness the confrontation.

By nine o'clock the yard was full and more people were coming through the door. Scorpio was getting hot with Johnny Osbourne's 'Reasons' and 'Show Me Your Sign'. After an hour, the current went over to Jammy. Wise Tupps opened right away with 'Sleng Teng' and the crowd went wild! People were cheering and throwing their hands in the air, blowing noise-makers and whistles. The bass sound that was coming out of those boxes was like nothing that had ever been heard before. It was absolutely clean – powerful and pounding. It just stopped your heart. And it had all come out of a 'music box', as the unfamiliar electronic keyboards were referred to then. Tupps was putting on Sugar Minott's 'War and Crime' when suddenly the melody was interrupted by the entrance of armed police officers, M16s on their shoulders. For over an hour the dance had to stop while police ordered everyone to the side as they searched each person, one by one, for weapons. John Wayne was heard to say something unacceptable about the police over the mike and was hauled off (he later returned intact).

Finally, after a luckily fruitless search, the officers retreated (with a few timid patrons) and the clash proceeded, but the verdict was already in – 'Sleng Teng' had won the day. What was it about a chance combination on a tiny Casio keyboard that could mesmerise an entire nation and change forever the course of reggae music? Once this 'computer' rhythm appeared, there was no turning back. Even Jammy had to reluctantly shelve over fifty 'human' rhythms he had made with the High Times band and not used yet, because no one wanted to hear them. All they wanted was 'Sleng Teng' – literally. Album after album of pure 'Sleng Teng' versions were released and every single one sold. It was Jammy's very first number one record in Jamaica (although he had had several abroad). Yes, 'the "Sleng Teng" dominate bad, bad,' as Tupps recalls.

Jammy's crew loading the truck for the clash

Jah Screw —
selector for
Black Scorpio

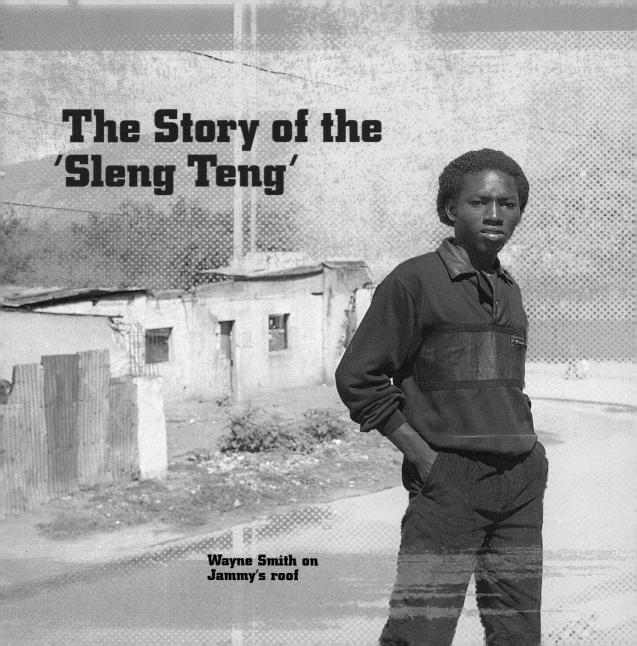

The Story of the 'Sleng Teng'

Wayne Smith on Jammy's roof

The story of how the 'Sleng Teng' rhythm was born must begin with singer **Wayne Smith** who helped it come into being. Born on December 5, 1965, Wayne and his five brothers and sisters grew up in Waterhouse. Wayne sang at school and at the Church of God and eventually learned electrical engineering at Papine, but Wayne wanted to sing. He hung around Jammy's sound until he got a hearing. And from the response, he was able to start making records. The first record Jammy did with Wayne was 'Ain't No Me Without You' in 1980. In 1982, Jammy produced an LP called *Youthman Skanking* that was only released abroad. After the LP, Wayne broke with the boss and spent some time working with Channel One (he can be heard on several of their one rhythm compilations of that time). In 1984, however, he was back with the King recording 'Ain't No Meaning' and 'Come Along'.

In those days of hanging around the music spots of Waterhouse, Wayne came in contact with Noel Dailey. Dailey owned one of those Casio 'Music Boxes', which was essentially a cheap keyboard. Noel was trying to make it as a singer and he used the box to help him practice. One day after one of these rehearsals, as Wayne remembers, 'On turning on the box, we came across a rock rhythm and decided to slow it down. After that I started to sing on the rhythm. We then lost the rhythm and could not find it again in the box. Noel was determined to find it and spent days until he located the rhythm. This time we made no mistake and went straight to Jammy's. The words of 'Sleng Teng' just leapt into my mind and the song was done.'

It was actually Tony Asher who laid down the final track for the recording. Tony was one of the few musicians currently doing a lot of session work who was comfortable with the electronic keyboards and who owned one. Until others were found, Asher had to handle the computer business almost single-handedly as the boom hit. By September of 1985, there was proof of at least two hundred 'Sleng Teng' versions for sale, and it didn't stop there. It hasn't even stopped now. Rhythm tracks are still appearing everyday that are only one step removed from that original creation. Songs like Pinchers' 'Agony' are still just a reworking of the 'Sleng Teng' idiom. That one rhythm had a truly revolutionary effect on reggae. And what a godsend it was for the independent producers that didn't own their own studios. Even Jammy could lay down his own rhythm tracks in that tiny bedroom in the back of the house, even though it could just barely hold two musicians and a mixer. The savings in money and convenience in both studio time and musicians' fees were incredible. No more delays at the studio. You never had to leave home. Even that wouldn't have been enough if the public didn't want it – but they did, like crazy. Credit must go to Jammy himself for being willing to try something new; Jammy kept himself surrounded with the youth vibes and knew what the people wanted.

Bobby Digital

His new mixer was a youth named Bobby, soon to be called 'Digital' after his role in mixing the computer hits became known. 'One of the quickest learning guys' Jammy had 'ever met,' Bobby had a feel for the new and exciting. He became the King's acknowledged 'right hand man'. As Jammy said, 'He can do everything on there just like myself.' Jammy was enthusiastic about Bobby's dedication and his obvious willingness to work hard and to work long hours if necessary (as it usually was). Already well acquainted with technician work, Bobby became the crucial cog in the wheel, the key to the whole operation. As Jammy's enterprise expanded, he was getting busy with business, having to travel frequently, and spending a lot more time on the road. But Bobby could fill in anywhere. He cut dub, mixed music, laid rhythms, auditioned and voiced artists. Of course Jammy had the final say, but Bobby was starting to lay the groundwork more and more.

Bobby had first found his way to the studio through a friend of his who had worked with Jammy clearing his things at airport customs – things like new equipment that required some delicacy in negotiation with the officers. As Bobby started coming around with his friend, he soon got to know the crew, and he slowly became fascinated by the whole operation. One day he was hanging around the place and Jammy was inside cutting some dub. Jammy got called away for a moment and when he returned, he found his son John John completing the work for him. As Tupps recalls, 'The dub was finished and John John take it off and turn it over the next side and put down the needle to cut it. And when Jammy come, Jammy was so surprised that his son can cut dub.' When Bobby, who witnessed the scene, saw that even Jammy's son could cut dub, he got jealous and decided he would learn it too, and the mixing as well. Jammy began teaching him the whole business. 'In the night', Tupps continues, 'when everybody supposed to be in bed – Jammy was a man like this, used to wait till everybody sleeping – he mixes albums. Bobby Digital used to observe, watching how he catch the levels, cause the first thing you have to do is catch the level. And from that time Jammy could rely on him to mix the tune and take a voice.'

Bobby Digital and Cocoa Tea mixing

Steely and Clevie
and Squingey

The remaining portion of the new computer crew was the dynamic duo, Steely and Clevie, the two men who have handled almost every Jammy rhythm track from 1985. The other keyboard whiz who often jammed with them was Pablo Black. Steely and Clevie are as familiar now as a pair to mechanised music as Sly and Robbie were to human sounds (although Sly and Robbie are no strangers to the new technology!), but it was Steely and Clevie who ruled dancehall. Steely Johnson had come to the Roots Radics band from the Generation Gap in the early 80s. This made him part of the dancehall scene immediately, as the Radics were the first session band to define the new style. His keyboard work had already been making hits for years when he joined Jammy's crew. Clevie (Cleveland Browne) had been a drummer at Studio One where he also played on many hits with artists like Freddie McGreggor, Johnny Osbourne, and Jennifer Lara. The musical Brown family also included Dalton. When Squingine Francis (Squingey) came up to Waterhouse from Maxfield, the studio crew was complete. Squingey, long famous as the dubcutting whiz kid from Channel One, was out of a job when the studio started losing business around that time. The Hookim brothers weren't around much anymore. Jo Jo was spending almost all his time at his pressing plant in New York where he took orders for small-run, custom presses. He came down regularly to repair equipment and collect the money from the jukebox concessions, but he wasn't really enthusiastic about the Jamaican end of the business.

Squingey cutting dub at Channel One

Pompidou voicing and
Squingey mixing at
Jammy's studio while
Screwdriver looks on

After a brief burst of prominence with their one-rhythm compilation LPs, they wound down to a halt. Talk was rife about their opening a new studio uptown; Jo Jo said they had even found the property and would begin building soon. But nothing ever materialised and business at Maxfield dropped off sharply. The pressing plant closed, the dubcutting room was locked. People still booked the studio, but with the computer style so much space wasn't really necessary. Only those true fans of the place – producers like Winston Riley and Junior Delgado who loved that certain special sound that only Channel One could give – kept buying time. So Squingey, the little, round mischief-maker, had to find a new home. He quickly adjusted to life in Waterhouse and seemed much more in his element than he ever did at Channel One. He got responsibility in the studio and learned the mixing part as well. He got a chance to experiment with making his own rhythms, and strolled around the grounds looking grandly pleased with himself for his new position. Squingey became popular in the area right away. He was friendly and helpful to everyone. Wycliffe Messam, Iris' nephew and record producer, remembers Squingey as 'a fun guy to have around. I remember the time I used to be down there and nobody would do my work for me and he always volunteered,' he remembers. 'When we feel hungry we would go the Kentucky [Fried Chicken] cause he loves Kentucky – that's his specialty. I really miss him.'

Squingey died in April 1988, quite suddenly. One day his belly swelled up and shortly thereafter he was dead. It was a terrible shock to the whole crew and to everyone around the world who knew him as a lively, impish, funny, and generous youth.

Purpleman and
Tullo T at the Shock
of the Century

The Four Sound Clash

Since 'Sleng Teng' had made the dance hot again and the return of the King had made competition heat up between sounds, a giant Four Sound Clash (to be held at the drive-in theatre Cinema Two) was planned for the spring. The promoter was Laing, a policeman and record producer (his label was Supreme, shared with MC Tommy Cowan). The line up was to be Jammy, Black Scorpio, Youth Promotion, and Arrows. Tension had been building all year between Jammy and Youth Promotion with charges and countercharges of borrowing, stealing, and copying various rhythms and lyrics passing back and forth. It was easy for things to get mixed up in a small city with an even smaller musical elite in which many singers and deejays travelled easily between the two sounds and labels. But in the sound business, competition is serious, and small things can turn into large things by way of rumour and tale, growing more extreme with each telling.

Pompidou and Twitch at a Jammy's dance

The Four Sound Clash, dubbed the 'Shock of the Century', took place on June 2 at Cinema Two. Inside the huge cement-floored area, four miserably small stages were set up in row against the back wall. The first belonged to Arrows, with Peter Metro and Joe Mannix. No one really knew why Arrows was there, as it didn't have the name at that time. It was still best known as the sound from St. Thomas that Yellowman had come up with. Rumours told that several other sounds had backed down for various reasons so Arrows had to fill in. Metro salvaged the night though, as he is always an immensely popular deejay in Kingston and has a tremendous following of his own through his Metromedia sound work. Second in the line came Black Scorpio with, of course, General Trees and company. His act was programmed like a slick stage show. Trees came right out early dressed head-to-toe in gray leather with his two sidekicks in full jockey regalia. They did the horseman move all night long, one on either side, while Trees went straight through every lyric he knew with incredible energy and drive. Lady G, who had turned into one of the better female deejays, took a few turns at the mike too. It was the only appearance of a woman at any stage that night.

Next came the King. Purpleman, another Waterhouse man, was one of the first to appear along with the horsemen. Soon Tullo T, Nitty Gritty, and Pompidou were up there rocking. Then came Chakademus, Tonto Irie, and John Wayne and the place was going crazy and gunshots were flying through the air overhead. The Johnny Osbourne dubplates were mashing down the place. The only problem was that some of Jammy's best singers never appeared; luckily, the deejays carried the night with ease.

Youth Promotion had the most crowded stage of all. All together, packed in tight, were Yami Bolo, Sugar, Thriller, Dickie, Ranking, Colourman (the bible preacher), Jackie Knockshot, Blacka T, Daddy Ants, Tenor Saw, and even a few more. Sugar was moving through his classic tunes, throwing out a line or two and letting the youth fill in the rest. Jackie Knockshot was licking his World War II sound effects while Major Stitch was pulling up Sugar's new computer tracks. A man was standing behind Sugar firing his gun into the air and nearly blasting Sugar's eardrums. Then the whole process started again from the beginning. But when it came time for Scorpio to play, the sound was chipping out. After several attempts, the sound just wouldn't start up, so Jammy just turned on the current and threw down a new special with Tenor Saw that said, 'Ring the alarm, another sound is dying.' That made the crowd go mad. Jammy was immediately into the lead, way ahead. From that moment, the sound men never let up. Tupps went through the Johnny Osbourne special 'In the Area' and 'Buddy Bye', and then on to the Nitty Gritty songs 'Trial and Crosses' (the Jammy version), and 'Jammy in Your Minty'. The crew was inspired. Chakademus was his silliest, Pompidou his most gravely-voiced – although then he called it a 'computer voice'. A Junior Reid plate was saying 'Jammy no borrow dub' when Tonto Irie had to stop the music and beg the crowd to ease off the stage, as every minute more and more fans were climbing up to participate. 'Watch them a run, Papa Jammy a come... one a penny hot cross buns,' a Tenor Saw plate introduced each member of the crew in song, and Chakademus responded with his 'Two Foot Walk' lyrics. After that he chanted: 'What a thing when you can't ride a rhythm' over 'Roll Call', and Nitty Gritty started improvising 'Hog Ina Your Minty'. 'Jammy ina your minty,' he sang over the 'Ain't No Meaning' rhythm, 'and him a root out your dubplate.' The performances all around were so fine that public opinion, the following day, had to call a tie between Jammy and Promotion and leave it at that. And life returned to normal – for a while.

Junior Reid

Fit You Have
Fe Fit

Back in Waterhouse, the big news was their own son, Junior Reid, join in Black Uhuru to replace Michael Rose who left right after the group won a Grammy Award. Rose was also a crucial part of Waterhouse history and the early days of the band's rehearsing there probably goes a fair way to explain that 'Waterhouse' sound that so many singers have. The new Uhuru had just released their first 45, 'Fit You Have Fe Fit', with a picture sleeve showing Junior, Uma, and Ducky on exercise cycles. For days, the jukebox of the bar on West Bay Farm Road near the bus stop blasted the song over and over – for days! Michael Rose and Ducky could be seen sitting on the ledge along Penwood Road. So much for the fame going to their heads – they looked Waterhouse born and bred and proud of it. Junior Reid, too, was all around Waterhouse, especially at Jammy's. He had grown up on St. Lucia Road himself, right across the street.

Junior had a familiar name abroad but he had yet to make a huge local hit. That came with the release of 'Foreign Mind' on Sugar Minott's Youth Promotion label. The success of the song not only inspired a lot of similar 'Foreign Mind' lyrics (as well as a new slang term for people who forget about their culture and long for American goods and lifestyles), it also became the basis for the first roots video. The production was all done by Jah Wise Promotions, a local Jamaican company. This new fame was cemented directly with the release of *Boom Shaka Lack*, an LP produced by Jammy and released abroad by Greensleeves. It featured some great material like 'Cross the Border', 'Mother Move', and the title song.

Cocoa Tea

So Junior was becoming a very hot item when he was invited to join the Grammy winners. It had been rumoured that Don Carlos was a contender for the job (as he was another popular singer with that special 'Waterhouse' style), but Junior won and gave the group a new image that was more youthful and enthusiastic, less militant and bitter. With Junior, the group lost the 'bite' but gained spontaneous energy and a new sense of fun. 'Fit You Have Fe Fit' reached the international crowd while losing nothing in the dancehall. Soon every deejay had 'fit' lyrics and Josie Wales was growling 'Fit you have fe fit, you have fe fit to come to Jammy's.'

Something awful started happening to the radio in Jamaica. 1986 opened with some drastic changes – much for the worse. The effervescent and flirtatious Bev Binns could no longer be heard crooning along with Cocoa Tea's 'Sonia' (her favourite) and Winston Williams, the 'Conscious One', was gone. Thus was lost the majority of the air-time locally-produced records could enjoy. Both personalities had given much attention to roots and dancehall music and their enthusiasm had been contagious. They made hits, popularised artists, and did the whole recording industry a great service. Their replacements were a sorry crew: light classics and an incongruous show of old rock hits that featured all the music we have always tried to hide from, like 'In-A-Gadda-Da-Vida'.

Instead of Miss Binn's lively local humour, we heard only affected foreign accents and few feeble attempts at jokes: 'The show features the Mighty Diamonds live, in concert – well of course they're live, they're in concert! Ha ha.' Barry G still kept his 'Two to Six Supermix' time slot that provided a small oasis in an ever-spreading desert of local music. Gregory Isaacs' small African Museum shop on Chancery Lane was boarded up and Joe Gibbs' shop, around the corner on Parade, had become a grocery store.

Another Four
Sound Clash

Yet excitement was still in the air, for another clash was coming. This time it was serious. The four sounds in the lineup were to be Jammy, Youth Promotion, Black Scorpio, and Black Star. Things were getting tense and some rivalries were flaring up again. Jackie Knockshot found himself caught right in the middle.

Jackie is proud to demonstrate how his removable front tooth enhances his ability to create unique sound effects through vocal improvisation. The tooth was lost in school, where war would break out every day at noon. As soon as lunchtime was called, the children would line up on either side of the schoolyard and bombard each other with rocks. So Knockshot turned necessity to talent and became a shotmaster. Jackie wasn't the first man to lick shots. That honour must go to Joe Lickshot, who began his career with Gemini sound imitating various gun noises with deadly accuracy. But Knockshot developed the comic side of the art and added Japanese sword clashes, WWII bombing raids, and even entire scenarios such as a patty race and his special CN News highlights that announced all the local gossip after the fashion of TV presenters.

Knockshot got involved with the dance business with Youth Promotion when he was living with his baby mother on Macdonald Avenue, next door to Barry Brown and not far from Robert Crescent. The problems arose when he left and returned to his mother's tiny home on Pennwood Avenue just north of the number 40 bus terminus in Waterhouse. His growing popularity ensured he would be desired by sounds to nice up the dance. Although Sugar had been the first man to put him on record with his famous introduction to Sugar's version of 'War and Crime', members of Jammy's crew soon began to court him, claiming him now as a Waterhouse resident and demanding his loyalty. So Knockshot began to feel himself under pressure. One day he would claim he was going to get a little room of his own on MacDonald Lane (where he could easily find one for forty or fifty dollars a month) and draw his cartoon in peace, but back in Waterhouse he would declare that Jammy's really needed him and so forth. By the day of the clash, he still hadn't decided on where to place his talent.

Youth Promotion was still resident at Robert Crescent and playing the sound in the yard every Thursday night, but Jammy was starting to expand the premises. Sugar's most worthy intention of developing young singers was backfiring as the successful ones left him for bigger producers with more ready cash instead of remaining to build up the sound. Thus, with all his sincere belief in his little operation, Sugar was losing ground to the highly competitive Jammy's complex. Jammy had all the overseas connections wrapped up and was developing a system of selecting one artist at a time to groom for success through the release of 45s and LPs, as well as videos, overseas shows, and through exposure on the sound itself.

Soon, the clash was the only topic of conversation in town. Sugar flew off to Miami to cut his dubs in secrecy, and Jammy's crew was carefully watching the gate to make sure no informers passed through. Had it not been for the growing popularity of Tiger, Black Star's special deejay with an entirely new style, the clash would certainly have been put down as just another contest between Jammy and Youth Promotion. But many people had never seen Tiger before and there was great curiosity about him. They had heard some of his bizarre lyrics like 'And when the friars come [to the dance] we lick them down – wind them up and make them move like robot.' Tiger was just plain different.

The excitement grew as representatives from the sounds appeared on TV and radio interviews that were seen and heard across Jamaica. The clash was to be held March 1 at Cinema Two. Jackie Knockshot, still afraid to show his face to either side, arrived quietly to take his place as an observer. He saw Admiral Bailey take the mike, surrounded by Don Angelo, Chakademus, Woody Noble, John Wayne, Tupps the selector, and Chris the mixer. Bailey was chanting: 'Politician me no like politician/ Kingston City Admiral come from/A no anything cook a restaurant nyam/Moveable man, I am a moveable man.' Jackie Knockshot takes up the narrative to explain the eventful night:

After one hour of playing, Jammy turn off his amps, but Black Scorpio sound could not be heard in the big open place at Cinema Two. Black Scorpio sound wasn't playing good so him decide to make Black Star play with Tiger, Bruck Back. Bruck Back take the mike first to thrill the public: 'A me name Bruck Back. A me name Bruck Back.' Soon afterward Black Star sound was giving technical problems. After, Black Star operator announce that Black Star have to stop playing for the night.

Colourman lead the Promotion Posse onstage to start the first round: 'Back to the bible.' Colourman was the God disciple, so all he do as a deejay is preach the gospel: 'Bible is a book everyman supposed to use, that is the book man nowadays refuse.' Then Tenor Saw took the mike: 'I love how Youth Promotion sound is playing.' Then Yammy Bolo: 'When a man's in love.' Due to technical problems, three sounds was not playing good – Youth Promotion, Black Star, and Black Scorpio. So Jack from Black Scorpio and Sugar were talking to each other. 'Hey Sugar, them pin me wire. We burn up Sugar, is what a gwan?' Sugar answer him back on the mike: 'Jack them pin me box too. Me a beg unoo, me can't buy another sound – don't pin me box!' Then Black Star them talk: 'Crowd a people, Black Star stop play for the night! The man them wan burn up the sound.' So only Jammy and Youth Promotion was left standing with Youth Promotion fading with all sorts of problems.

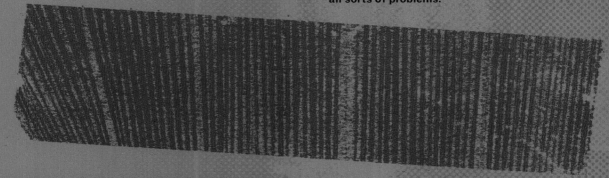

By then the crowd start yelling: 'Jammy's! Jammy's!'
For a long time is was pure talking and complaining.
Jammy played the first round without any bugs, no
slip ups. At that time Promotion was fixing a wiring
on the amps and so Jammy seizes the opportunity
and start yelling: 'Well, Sugar, your time fe play
is up. Everyman have a certain time fe play.' Tupps
touch down with Johnny Osbourne's 'Ooooooo what
a la la, Papa Jammy in the area.' John Wayne eat
up the 'Stalag' rhythm: 'Hey – ready fe we, them no
ready fe we.' After, Pompidou [and] Chakademus
speak: 'Now Youth Promotion we and you – one
selection to end.' So Youth Promotion was given
a chance to play again. So Major Stitch, the
selector, put on a Superblack: 'You trying to conquer
Promotion.' After that Major Stitch put on a King
Kong selection with Jackie Knockshot on the intro:
'The way between me and the old pan sound have
to over.' There was all kinds of massive at Cinema
Two – Spanglers, Bounty Hunters, One A Penny,
Junglist, Paynelandites. One of the Jammy deejays
push Yami Bolo off the stage and bottle start throw
from the two sides. Chakademus was hit.

Disaster strike at Cinema Two. People start running;
many people were hurt, some were trampled.
Everyone was panicking. Deejay have to run. Soon
after the noise stop. Then it was told: 'Is a guard
leggo a horse station dog to run down a man.' One
hundred pairs of shoes were found and presented
on stage for their owners. Gold chain were reported
to have stolen in the crowd. All sound men have to
secure their amps and boxes. Some of Sugar Minott's
boxes were pushed down. Then the worst thing
happened: the police say they saw two wanted man
in the dance and was searching for them. The two
jump the wall and make their escape in the gully.
Back at Cinema Two, some supporter grab the
trophy that was to be presented to the winner of the
contest and start yelling. Pity they didn't know that
the contest was judged by four categories. The
points were: the sound that play the best, the most
discipline group, the most conscious lyrics, the best
selection, and it resulted with King Jammy winning
two points, Black Star best conduct group, Youth
Promotion the most conscious lyrics. Well, Black
Scorpio came last.

Jackie Knockshot finally resolved his difficulties
by flying out for a tour of some Caribbean Islands
and eventually settling down in New York, up
in Spangler's territory, Manhattan, where he was
close to Jah Wise and made frequent trips out to
Brooklyn to nice up New York dances. Jammy
had emerged from the clash with the trophy, but
the events of the night left bitterness and confusion,
so that was the last heard about such massive
competitions from then on.

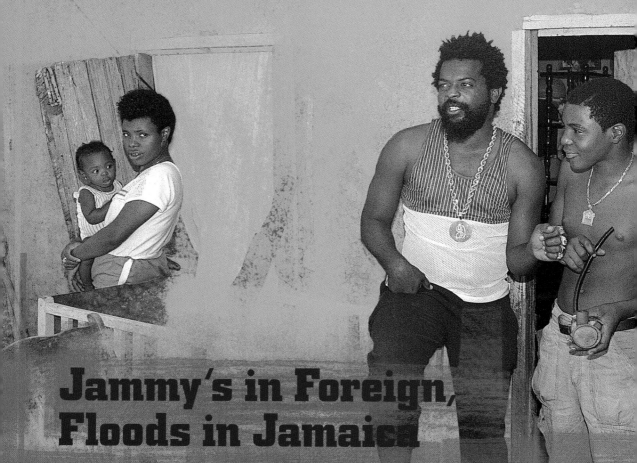

Junior Delgado
and Yammy Bolo

Jammy's in Foreign,
Floods in Jamaica

The next month, the sound crew left the island for a long tour of the New York area with dates in Jersey, Philadelphia, and Washington, D.C. The only deejays that went on this trip were Chakademus, Tonto Irie, and John Wayne, but they were joined in every city by other top entertainers, either resident or visiting. The first object was to throw down the reigning New York champion, Downbeat. Downbeat had traditionally been home to the top travelling entertainers and was always host to Brigadier when he was in the area, but Jammy's emerged from the clash triumphant with his special music. Reports give credit to 'Jammy's Got the Title' by Pad Anthony; his classic, international dubplate on the 'General' rhythm. The rhythm wasn't new then, and isn't now, but it always gets a sure crowd response.

In preparation for the tour, sponsor Salbo and Jammy got a pattern made up and began printing King Jammy's official T-shirts, sweatshirts, and tour jackets. These were manufactured in New York by Extetics International. To this catalogue of Jammy-wear has been added caps, dresses, and tracksuits, which are only available through Jammy in Jamaica or Messam in Canada. They are mainly made to order for special events, and whatever's left over is sold through the studio in Kingston.

June in Jamaica brought the devastating floods that left so many homeless and wiped out miles of cropland. Cocoa Tea memorialised the incident in his song: 'On the sixth of the sixth, nineteen eighty-six.' Actually, June 6 was the first day the sun could be seen after two and a half weeks of rain. That was the day the flood-waters stopped and finally began to recede and the government was able to go into the areas to assess the damage.

Jammy and crew were still abroad, although rumour had them returning each day, always the next day. The flood hadn't affected Kingston directly, but the constant rain had completely destroyed what little surfacing there had been on the city roads, leaving dirt and stones and broken chunks of paving in its place. Driving was worse than impossible, and even walking raised a cloud of dust that obscured visibility. What Kingston did feel, however, was the shortage of ganja that the flood left. Not only had entire fields been wiped out, but the roads going out to those parts were unserviceable. Nothing was getting through and prices began to rise in accordance with the demand. The only consolation was the World Cup Soccer Championship. Anyone with a TV set had a certain crowd of people in their house daily and often the streets looked deserted for the duration.

With the crew gone, things were quiet, but business went on as usual at the studio. Iris, Bobby, and Bravo were away with the crew, so Squingey was left in charge of the dubcutting and he was working on some plates of Nitty Gritty's 'Cry Baby', a much punchier dubplate mix than the version on the LP, as well as Don Angelo's 'Petty Robber'. Meanwhile, the construction in the yard was underway. A friend of Iris' had informed Jammy that the house next door to him was up for sale, and nothing could have been more opportune. Jammy bought the property immediately and tore down the wall in between. Jammy was expanding.

A lot of sounds had been forced to stop playing during the rains, so a lot of the entertainers were walking around broke. Everyday the radio announced new benefits to be held in support of the victims.

It was the year of 'Boops' in the music world, but it was about to become the 'Raggamuffin' year. The Taxi 45s with Half Pint, 'Night Life Lady' and 'Cost of Living', had been released but the rhythms were just too complex, too structured to play well at dances. Instead it was the driving rhythms of 'Greetings' on George Phang's Powerhouse label (also a Sly and Robbie effort) that caught on. The message was one that every ghetto dweller could identify with.

Junior Delgado followed up with his 'Raggamuffin Year' – 'Raggamuffin year is here, revolution year, coming here' – and the new craze was launched. Junior had made quite a comeback after re-settling in his homeland. His long absence in England had kept him musically inert for a while, but he proved that he could create not only hits, but some very sophisticated, creative music as well. Jammy's recording of 'Raiders', his original tune on the updated rhythm that was making the rounds that year, signaled his return. His LP with Jammy contained some of Steely and Clevie's most innovative work. The keyboards had lightened up from the solid 'Sleng Teng' pounding and became, at times, airy and enchanted. The computer business was reaching a stage of maturity.

When the tour finally did return from abroad, Jammy had something very special to announce: he and his babymother Iris – girlfriend of sixteen years – were going to get married. Iris remembers dating Jammy since her school days. They began going out when she was just thirteen and attending Denham Town School. Jammy was going to another school but they lived close by and saw each other often. Jammy was older but that was the custom in Jamaica, to start friendships early and young. The wedding was quite a lavish affair with the reception at Hope Gardens. A friend was playing a small sound – just soft music – and the food and drinks were overflowing. It was the big celebrity event of the season with every entertainer present. It made Iris, officially, Queen of Jammy's, and Jam II, a little prince.

Connections

The New York tour allowed Jammy to make another important connection. He found Count Shelley's new base, the re-activated Live and Love records in Brooklyn, New York, near Church and Utica. The old Live and Love label used to have some classics of the late 70s like all the Bunny Lee hits. Suddenly, after sheltering in the U.K. for a while, Shelley was back on the international scene. His huge record store outlet soon grew too small to handle his distribution business and he had to open a separate store for wholesale operations a block away. And the boost his label got was from Jammy's music! He got almost the whole lot of what was coming out on LPs and discos long before the songs were released on 45 (if ever) in Jamaica.

Whereas Greensleeves had released the Nitty Gritty LP in 1985, Shelley's Live and Love had gotten the first Junior Delgado in 1986, as well as the first King Kong LP, *Legal We Legal*. Shelly then left to England where he opened a distribution point over there. That gave him the widest latitude in getting music out quickly on both continents – exactly what Jammy wanted. Whereas Greensleeves had been careful in selecting one disco release at a time, Shelley had no scruples about rushing the music out right when it was freshest and hot. The combination worked wonderfully and gave Jammy the international exposure he so badly needed at the time.

Sales in Jamaica were going well too. The *Sunday Gleaner*, in a report on local figures, gave the totals for some of the top 45s of the year: Echo Minott's 'What the Hell' and 'Police in England' by Peter Metro had each sold 15,000 copies, while 'One Scotch, One Bourbon' by Admiral Bailey and Chakademus had sold 12,000.

Both Chakademus and Tonto Irie shared the spotlight as Jammy's star deejays, but both left the sound soon after. Tonto Irie had come to Jammy from Black Star in 1985. At Black Star he had served for years in the shadow of Brigadier, but at Jammy's he matured and developed his own style. When he left, it wasn't to work for another sound but to spend more time abroad, recording song like the great 'New York Life' for Music Master in New York, and working on live stage shows. He had reached the point where he was popular enough to freelance safely. Likewise, Chakademus, after the success of his combination tune with Bailey, teamed up with Errol Scorcher, an original Jammy deejay, to record together on their own. They did 'Miami Vice' at the height of the shorts and matching shirt fad, poking fun at the dandy Jamaican follower of fashion. Since this time, Chakademus has been freelancing and often travelling abroad to work shows in the States.

**Admiral
Bailey**

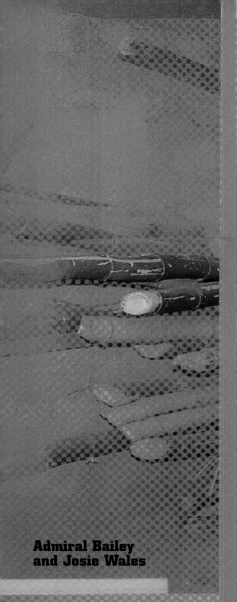

It was time for Jammy to bring forward a new star deejay and it looked like the one with the most potential was Admiral Bailey, as he had already gained a good following through the tune with Chakademus. This proved to be the right move, for Bailey hit almost immediately with 'Punaany', the 'not-fit-for-airplay' smash that set the trend for the rest of the year. With 'Punaany' and 'Two Year Old' for Jah Life, poor Admiral was topping the charts with two songs that had been banned from the radio. The problem was solved when he recorded 'Healthy Body', some very constructive lyrics on the 'Punaany' rhythm, and it soon started climbing the charts faster than the original. He commented: '"Healthy body" was made for radio purpose. I wasn't looking for that result ... Nuff people say me do "Healthy Body" better than "Punaany".'

It should have been obvious – anything Bailey did was bound to hit. His popularity had grown so large. When he did 'Big Belly Man', it went straight up the chart too. Luckily, it was fit for airplay. Artists who had spent the earlier part of the year answering 'Punaany' on record – and enough did to fill a few LPs – started in on the 'Big Belly' trend with all kinds of lyrics about 'Small Belly Men' and 'Long Belly Men'. But the best was still the original. It equated big bellies with money and power, making his own belly a topic to boast of, not hide, and listed all the famous big belly men in Jamaica.

**Admiral Bailey
and Josie Wales**

Bailey began his musical life growing up in Cockburn Penn where Stur-Gav used to play. He was an avid fan of Ranking Joe and used to learn by imitating Joe's fast-talking style. You can still hear the influence in the way Bailey projects his voice – loud and booming. At the time he found Jammy's he was living not far away at Olympic Way and Bay Farm Road, where Josie Wales was also to be found. Bobby Digital heard him at a dance out there and told Jammy about him and Jammy called him in right away. He was perfect for the Jammy's team. They needed a good talker with a strong voice. Tonto Irie had the lyrics, but his voice wasn't the best. Jammy's never went for the fancy-talking guys that could runaway at a thousand words per minute. He had the guys who could just ride a rhythm, steady and solid. Bailey matched Chakademus well.

Thus Bailey joined the sound and began recording for the King. He even teamed up with pal Josie Wales to make the controversial 'Ballot Box' to clear the air of rumours that the two had stolen a ballot box from a neighbourhood polling station in the recent local elections. They handled the situation with such tact and humour that the whole affair was soon dropped: 'Who say the Colonel, a who say the Admiral thief the ballot box?' they sang. 'Look how we big, look how we fat, how we fe jump fence, with ballot box?' Bailey was making it because he had all the key ingredients – a strong voice, good timing, and humour. Like his friend Josie, Bailey always tried to add a little comedy to his work, such as the story of how people in the district used to shun him when he was a dirty little ghetto youth. Now they all crowd around the star. Instead of using a self-pity delivery, Bailey teaches a good moral lesson with a laugh and gets a better result.

The other artist Jammy seemed to back for the year was singer Superblack, but this didn't work as well. The song 'Deh with You' was a promising start and Jammy released a nice LP with him, but surprise – Pinchers came along that year and wiped everybody out.

The streets of Kingston were looking remarkably clean. All the hagglers who used to line their stalls along Half Way Tree Road and Square had been moved to a brand new efficiency mall on Constant Spring Road. But despite the new drive to eliminate refuse from the streets and set up more garbage receptacles, the crime was growing steadily worse. Downtown Kingston was becoming a risky place. The corners – all four at Orange and North Streets (just above Pablo's little Rockers store) were covered in graffiti letters warning: 'Thieves Keep Out' and 'Vigilante Posse is watching you!' in a ghetto version of a Neighbourhood Watch program.

At Half Way Tree, the famous Skateland had returned to skating. The skates were back at last and people were rolling around the rink every night once again, amongst them many recording artists. Horace Andy, one of the biggest skate enthusiasts, had a new headquarters.

Expanding
the Business

Back at Jammy's, large-scale construction was underway. The door leading into the little studio was now enclosed in the shell of the new studio-to-be. The walls were up and a cement ledge had to be climbed over to reach the voicing room door where Squingey was cutting dub and Bobby was mixing. It was a little difficult to manoeuvre in the yard with all the blocks and building materials around, but watching the transformation was exciting.

What had been a small house in the yard next door was now Mama Iris' Beauty Parlour and it was taking customers in full operation. The other half of the house was still serving as a laundry room where an ironing board was set up. Facing the road and extending from the wall of this house to the wall of the yard was a twelve-foot high fence with a smaller door cut out through which people could be let through individually. This door was always kept locked and Boxer had the key. Sometimes Boxer couldn't be found and a big round of shouting would ensue as people searched for the gateman while the visitors were pounding on the gate. On the front of the house, Jammy's painter friend had perfectly lettered signs proclaiming it the home of Jammy's Superpower, without a doubt.

Boxer with Jam II
and another child

The rest of the yard behind the house served as a parking space for Jammy and his brother, Trevor, and as an area for the mechanic to work on their cars. The original house now has the studio shell attached behind it. At the back, the shed and office shared one roof. All are connected by way of an internal phone system that also touches the gate. The phone at the gate can also be used to page people through the **PA**.

The office, Trevor's domain, contained a video monitor as well. Jammy, when not on the road, patrols the yard with his cordless phone in his back pocket. Gone are the days when Iris had to struggle with a lock on their old-style, dialing model. Bravo always had the keys and no one could ever find him when a call was wanted. Yet somehow, long distance calls always showed up unwanted on the bills, no matter how carefully you kept the lock. Every musician had what they claimed was some sure formula for calling on a locked phone. Undoubtedly, some of them worked.

Little Jam II had just started school. Every morning he was dressed in a khaki suit and driven off. Johnny Clarke had returned, at last, from too many years abroad, and was recording some fresh material with Jammy. When his crisp red **BMW** car was on St. Lucia Road, Clarke was inside, still wearing his tall, felt hat; Josie Wales was working with the sound when he wasn't in demand for stage shows. He was wearing a real raggamuffin style with his hair in cornrows and his feet bare.

Pablo Black was in the studio filling in temporarily for Clevie, making new rhythms with Steely. On Saturdays, race day in Kingston, everyone would be sure to check with Pablo before placing a bet. He would lean against Jammy's car, racing form in his hand, and study it carefully before making any choice, but when he finally declared his favourite, he was invariably correct. The little restaurant down St. Lucia Road served as the neighbourhood betting shop and did a brisk business.

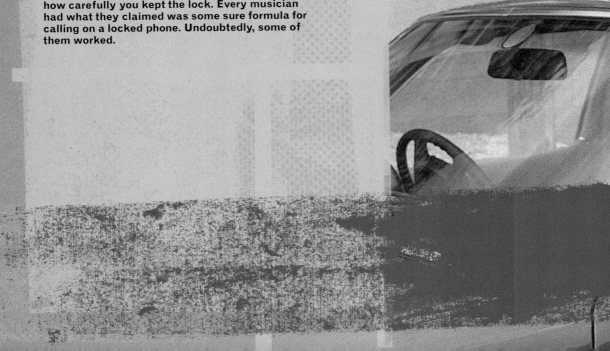

Johnny Clarke

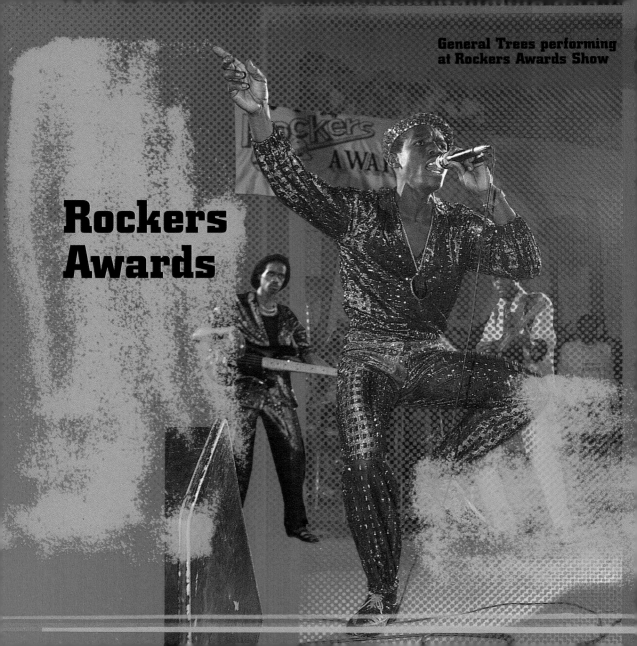

General Trees performing
at Rockers Awards Show

Rockers
Awards

The annual Rockers awards ceremony was held on January 31 to cover the year 1986. The National Area was filled as people came to see appearances by General Trees, Sophia George, Tiger, and Leroy Smart, all backed by the Rhythm Kings band. Various entertainers were arriving all night. The Jammy's posse made a grand entrance all together – and they were dressed to kill. Even Dummy Roy was decked out in a three-piece suit, looking every bit the gentleman.

The ceremony was difficult to follow, the sound not being up to par. It was difficult to understand the announcements and hardly anybody knew what the winners, who were presented on stage, were winning for. But the audience still proved a lively participant in the event. When Carlene Davis won the 'Best Dressed Award', the announcement was greeted with loud 'boooos' and 'no no' – after seeing Trees in his blue sequined track suit and Tiger in his red and black-checked gangster style.

Jammy won easily as the best producer but when it came to top sound system, a hostile crowd received the news that Classique, the soul and oldies sound, had won. The Jammy's posse still resents the affront. What was a soul sound doing in the 'Rockers' awards anyway? The year before, top sound had been by Kilamanjaro and Jaro hadn't even been playing that year. People doubted the critical abilities of the judging committee bitterly.

Still the awards had no effect on the public who continued to follow Jammy's as the reigning sound. New entertainers were gathering around Jammy everyday hoping for a piece of the big time action, hoping Jammy could make them a star. Newcomer Leroy Gibbons, after struggling to gain even the slightest recognition in Canada, had come to Waterhouse at last to try a new approach.

Many of the old Jammy's crew had faded away, making room for the new. Wayne Smith had disappeared into the States and released a 45 on his own Sleng Teng label. Tenor Saw was in New York, often going to Miami to record one or two songs for Skeng Man's Skengdon label. King Kong left Jamaica and never returned, dividing his time between England, Toronto, and New York. Nitty Gritty too had fled to England, occasionally surfacing in New York but keeping a low profile all around. Jammy, always looking for fresh talent, was happy to have new artists coming in. He began recording with Lieutenant Stitchie and Pinchers, the two superstars of 1987. And he began working steadily with all-time favourite Cocoa Tea. Next to 'Punaany', Pinchers' 'Agony' became the outstanding song of the time. It was a little slow in catching on but it made Pinchers the girls' pet. Not even Little John or Tristan Palma at their height could match the female madness that followed Pinchers. Every concert saw him backstage, trapped in a corner surrounded by adoring women, while the other artists were free to roam about. While 'Punaany' was slack, none of Pinchers' lyrics were rude enough to be banned, but they did reach the limits of suggestiveness. He did over his 'Sit Down Pon It' (originally done for Redman) for Jammy's and made it a new song; the rhythm was dynamic. He had previously recorded an LP for Vena, but he was sounding like Tenor Saw or Nitty Gritty and doing weak dancehall lyrics.

Pinchers with some friends hanging outside of Jammy's studio

Risto Benji with his crippled friend

It was with Jammy that his style matured, through a conscious decision Pinchers made to be himself. When he realised that the imitation style he had been assuming out of safety (as a newcomer to a competitive business) wasn't working, he reasoned: 'Let me be my own river, let me run in my own stream rather than following somebody else's... So I start to sing my own way, now, which I was singing before – Pinchers, originally, myself.' As a serious Christian boy who grew up attending Christian school, Pinchers' sensuality retains the innocence that drives girls crazy. He still sings about God, although it is in the same indirect, slightly camouflaged way he sings about sex. But the meaning is still there for the careful listener.

The sound had built up a very impressive working group of artists. Admiral Bailey was joined by fellow Cockburn Penn resident Little Twitch, who grew up near Josie, Willy, U-Roy and the Stur-Gav crew, bringing another bit of that solid style to Waterhouse. Anthony Malvo had come over from Black Star, a once-great sound that was slowly fading from view entirely. Josie still worked the sound when there. So did old reliables like Pompidou, Tullo T, and John Wayne – until his bike accident knocked him out of commission for several months. Wayne was alright, but still too unsteady to exert himself unnecessarily. New singer Colin Roach came with a smooth-sounding voice, close to Gregory Isaacs. Little Risto Benji, the then twelve-year-old, was really shocking out. Shabba Ranks was a new member, and so was a fellow named Gregory Peck. Tupps spent much of the year abroad, and his place as selector was temporarily taken by crewmember Nya.

King Jammy's
SUPER POWER **1**

King's

POWER 2

**Ninja and an
unknown child**

Mixer Chris was also absent a lot, so Ninja, a little boy they found on the north coast while playing a dance in Montego Bay, was brought in to help out. Sadly, Ninja was hit by a truck the following year and killed. The crew is looking forward to having Chris as a permanent member again. Nya had originally been brought into the selecting field as a second to Tupps – and deservedly so after Tupps' long career selecting for the dances all by himself. Nya was to play first, getting the people warmed up, and to learn the selecting trade so that he could take over in Tupps' absence. Benji had come into the Jammy family by being a neighbourhood kid. He lived around the corner with his mother. Since his father was shot and killed, Benji looked to Jammy as a father and Jammy took responsibility for him.

Messam remembers a dance in Montego Bay, the first time he heard little Risto. It was a clash with African Symbol: 'Yammy Bolo and White Mice were on the next sound with General Leon. So Jammy had Benji ready as a secret weapon. The people really love him.' That was a couple of years ago and Benji would have been only eleven. Even now, at thirteen, he is small for his age, just waist high to a man. But don't watch his size. His timing is uncannily accurate, he has the best natural rhythm of all the child deejay that have been presented over the years, and he doesn't have an obnoxious, high, squeaky voice. He sounds quite solid, though young. He doesn't have a ton of original lyrics – yet – but his delivery is good and he is going to be a very proficient adult. As a child, he is being rushed into the big time. He flies out regularly for dances and stage shows abroad. Jammy serves as his manager and conducts all his business. He makes some big money, but as Messam points out – even at thirteen – 'He's the only one out there supporting his family.' Whatever money doesn't go to buy batteries for his new remote control car must go back to his mother in Jamaica. Sometimes you just have to grow up fast. There isn't always time to be a child in Jamaica.

Police, Politics, and Worries

That spring brought an incredible heat wave to the island. Streets looked deserted as everyone stayed indoors, out of the sun, and close to an air conditioner if possible. A strange rumour that it was now a crime to hold a package of Rizla was making the rounds. Some say the rumour was planted by the government itself to discourage ganja smoking. The result was that street vendors, believing it to be illegal, stopped selling them. A shortage – a severe one – developed immediately and the bold higglers took control. The few who knew the law (and there had been no law made regarding the papers) knew it was no crime and proudly displayed their 'contraband' at highly inflated prices – like $5 or $6 a pack.

Power outages were being scheduled again and each morning the *Gleaner* would print a list of the areas to be relegated to darkness that day. The talk of an imminent election (which had been going on for years) was being raised again at massive political meetings all over the country. The JLP radio commercial attempted to get hip by using the version of 'What One Dance Can Do' and Arrows' 'Hot Hot Hot' to jazz up the message. The PNP were telling people to 'Come in your tens of thousands' – although there couldn't be an election until the enumeration was finished and it was still proceeding slowly. The enumerators had to call at every house and list each occupant, take a thumb print of each, and have each person's photo taken for the identification card.

The saddest event of the year was certainly the death of Jammy's upcoming superstar deejay, Major Worries. It is a great tribute to a deejay's talent when even the anti-talking, pro-singing parts of the public acclaim him, as they did. Messam, a man who only works with singers and hates all deejays, makes an exception for Worries. He was a man of a million styles. The closest deejay to him in history is another who died young – General Echo.

Major Worries

Like Echo, Worries could sing, slur, imitate women's voices, and imitate animal noises. He could tell a complete story in a song, not by cramming it full of words, but by using a touch of humour. The song 'Topa' is about drunk people (the English word is toper). 'Seems like Topa want to buy him liquor/ Seems like Topa sleep under counter.' Worries had joined Jammy's sound in 1985 but was here regularly the following year, which was also the year he started to record with Jammy. 'Topa' and 'Babylon Boops' (on a various artists' LP and a Live and Love disco) were released before his death, as was Jah Life's 45, 'Product Of Jamaica'. These records showed a deejay with incredible talent just on the verge of making a clean sweep of the scene. Worries' death was all the more tragic for the needless violence of it. He was shot to death in August by a policeman after he had intervened in an argument the policeman was having with a friend of Worries.

The community in Spanish Town, where Worries lived and where the incident occurred, was so outraged that they mounted roadblocks of cars and tires that prevented traffic from moving in or out of the city.

Recordings with Worries were still coming out a year after his death. Redman released 'Hunter's Crossing', Scorpio had 'Run Down Money', Jah Life released 'Doo Doo' and had a full LP to follow, and France label had 'Mek Some Money' (where he barks like a dog). Other Worries tunes can be found on the Jah Life various artists' LP, *Works For The Future*. There's also 'Take You Eye Off Me', the Jammy's 'Superstar Hit Parade', 'Twist a Rock', and Micron's various artists' 'Talk Till She Hoarse'. Other 45s include Jammy's 'Me No Response' and two earlier Lightning 45s, 'Freezone' (with Little Tenna) and 'Ku Pon You'.

Although Worries had performed in Canada before, his first big outing abroad was to be with the official Jammy's tour that was to touch Toronto, England, and the States. The first step was Canada in October. Tupps and Nya had both come to select, along with Bailey, Twitch, Risto, Malvo, Collin Roach, Tullo T, Chuck Turner, and Bobby Digital, later to be joined by Iris and Trevor.

The first night was naturally a jam-packed affair with hoards of people crowding the steps and trying to push their way in, but there were ominous signs. There was no metal detector at the door (a requisite tool for Toronto dances) and the beer was being served in bottles. That left wide-open the possibilities for disaster. The crowd inside made a circle around the area in front of the stage where the sound was set up, mesmerised by little Risto dancing around and chanting. He and Tullo and Colin Roach handled the warm up before the big name artists were to appear on the stage. Plenty of video camera were going and the floor of the hall was crisscrossed with thick power cords. Twitch opened up the stage show part and the audience was getting excited. Finally, Bailey came in and crept along the back of the stage, outside of the spotlight, to await his turn. The crowd, however, saw him, and started going wild.

But just as Bailey was to take the mike, the sound suddenly chipped out. It seems that too much power was being drained with all the video machinery, and the hall couldn't handle it. Things were getting tense. Then the first beer bottle went crashing to the floor with a sound so closely resembling a gunshot that the crowd began to stampede. Naturally, the hall had not adequate exits, so people were huddled into every corner. Soon, they slowly began to come out, but when a second noise was heard the crowds scattered violently, luckily injuring no one. The sound was still off and people began to wander outside the front exit to wait where it was safer. Or so they thought. That's when a man appeared on the stairs firing a gun. Everyone went sprinting down St. Clair Avenue and running up side streets. The gun went off again. People continued running until they were far out of reach and the dance was over, another victim of irresponsible promoting. That incident effectively spoiled the tour for the crew so they wrapped it up early and went back to Jamaica to prepare for England.

The new year, 1988, brought a rest for the sound but an equal increase in recording activity. Jammy was putting out hits one after another with confidence and ease. The Frankie Paul LPs, *Sara* and *Casanova*, were cleaning up while his LP with Lieutenant Stitchie got Atlantic records so interested that they signed him to a five record deal, an unheard of signal of the music's viability. Since Yellowman had gotten in with a gimmick before being dumped by major CBS, no deejay had come close to attracting the attention of a major record label. Also, Jammy's Johnny Clarke LP was doing well and his Gergory Isaacs' album was said to be Gregory's best work by far in a very long time. Jammy's secret weapon for 1988, however, was Leroy Gibbons, the Canadian singer who had to come to Jamaica to get recognition in his own right.

Admiral Tibett

When the Rockers Awards time rolled around again,
Jammy and his crew got the recognition they had
been working for. Jammy won clear for best producer
for 1987 and tied Stone Love for best sound. Admiral
Bailey won best deejay and best reggae 45 with
'Big Belly Man'. Pinchers and Lieutenant Stitchie
shared new artist of the year and Steely and Clevie
got best instrumentalists. A good showing indeed.

After the Christmas season, and all the big dances
that come with it, the sound went on a little vacation.
All the artists were dismissed to freelance or loaf
and the technicians went to work clearing out the
bugs. The sound had begun to develop some top end
trouble. The tweeters were blowing out and needed
an overhaul.

There were also problems with police closing down
dances due to a rash of noise complaints from people
living in the area where the sounds were playing.
City laws on allowable noise levels after certain
hours were consulted and used as a reason to close
down sounds. So, it was time to just cool out and
work towards the future. The future had in store a
big, huge comeback stage show and dance scheduled
for the Easter weekend. Jammy's Tenth Anniversary
Hit Parade took place on Saturday, April 2 at
Cinema One with every Jammy artist plus all the
best of the rest.

White Mice

The Jammy's family was starting to branch out. Both Bobby Digital and Steely and Clevie formed their own labels. Bobby had been experimenting in the studio for years making his own rhythms, so he was experienced. The first releases on the Digital B label were Admiral Tibett's 'Too Much Jealousy' and Flourgon and Daddy Lizard's 'Jump and Spread Out'. Steely and Clevie started with the hilarious 'Bruk Camera' with old-timer Dillinger and Courtney Melody and 'No Free Ride' with Techniques' deejay, Johnny P. A new engineer, Mikey, came into the studio to meet the growing workload.

Jammy himself no longer lives in the little house on St. Lucia Road in the room in front of the studio. He and Iris and children have finally been able to purchase a nice place out in Hope Pastures, just past Barbican, near the Botanical Gardens. The children, who grew up in Waterhouse surrounded by the often-wild brand of artists so common in reggae, will have a chance to see that another style of life is possible. It's not easy to leave the ghetto in Jamaica. It's almost impossible, but Jammy got out. He no longer lives in the centre of the ghetto, but his roots are still there and they will always be in Waterhouse. He's there at the studio everyday, and Iris too. The music, and the ghetto that goes with it all, is his life and he can't leave that, ever.

Afterword

At the time it was first published in autumn 1989, not many more than a thousand copies of *King Jammy's* were ever printed. So, few people outside of a small network of reggae fans actually got to read Beth Lesser's book the first time around. Since Bob Marley's death in 1981, the wider world had generally forgotten about reggae, and there was a commonly held view that the music had somehow 'died' with him. This book eloquently discloses another, more optimistic, ultimately more truthful facet of Jamaican music history. Although the book is named after King Jammy, the story told here is not that of one man alone. Both figuratively and literally, it describes a whole family – not only Jammy's own, but also a bigger one of artists, engineers, deejays, selectors, gatemen, and ghetto dwellers – even the story of the 'box-lifters' who struggle with the giant speakers carried by any classic sound system is included. And during the period covered in this book, Jammy's Super-Power became the greatest. In these pages, the whole process of 'sound' in the Jamaican sense is laid bare.

What makes this book even more crucial is that Beth is describing Jamaican music history in the making; namely the arrival of the 'digital' sound in the Jamaican dancehall, in the form of the legendary 'Sleng Teng', and the circumstances surrounding its creation. Wayne Smith's 'Sleng Teng' has gone on to be the 7th most popular rhythm track in the history of the Jamaican dancehall. There are over 160 versions currently logged on the website www.reggae-riddims.com; theoretically this rhythm could be played for more than twelve hours without a break. Along with 'Punaany', Jammy's other major creation of the period, 'Sleng Teng' is the only digital rhythm among the top ten most-recorded. Thus, its arrival signaled the beginning of a new phase. It marks a dividing line between live instrumentation and 'digital' rhythms: before and after 'Sleng Teng'.

The development of Jamaican music is rooted in the runnings of the dancehall; this has been the case since the 1950s and remains true today. Throughout the music's history, certain producers and studios have come to dominate the scene, beginning with Clement 'Coxsone' Dodd's Studio One from the 1960s. When reggae arrived on the scene in 1968, Coxsone was still on top, having momentarily ceded his position to longtime rival Arthur 'Duke' Reid in the brief rocksteady era. Mr. Dodd still remains a major influence even today, but by the mid-70s the Waterhouse studio of the late dubmaster King Tubby was in control. From King Tubby's 'academy' came a new generation of engineers and producers, including not only Jammy, but also Hopeton 'Scientist' Brown, and 'Prince' Phillip Smart. Both of the latter apprentices went on to greater things. Scientist became the resident engineer at Channel One and Tuff Gong studios, where he worked until the mid-80s, and Prince Philip went on to found HCF, the leading U.S. reggae studio based in Long Island, New York. Prince Jammy, as he was then known, became a King in his own right, the greatest of all King Tubby's graduates, eventually occupying, for the digital generation, a position analogous to that of Coxsone Dodd in the music's genesis.

Jammy's studio, as described herein, became a breeding ground for some of the most successful artists and producers in Jamaican music right up to the present day. You can see even more of their names on the studio yard wall today than you can in Beth's pictures in this book. Jammy's assistant engineer, Bobby 'Digital' Dixon, became a brilliant producer in his own right – particularly strong when recording vocalists such as Cocoa Tea and Sanchez, and typified in his mid-90s revival of the traditional Rasta-style 'Kette Drum' rhythm. Jammy's then omnipresent studio musicians, Wycliffe 'Steely' Johnson and Cleveland 'Clevie' Browne, also soon branched out on their own, scoring hit after hit with deejays like Ninjaman and Cutty Ranks, as well as with vocalists, including veterans like Freddie McGregor alongside newcomers like Foxy Brown. The studio at 38 St. Lucia Road also served as a launchpad for the careers of several of the most successful deejays from the late 80s and early 90s, among them Lieutenant Stitchie, Admiral Bailey, Chakademus (who would later enjoy huge success with vocalist Pliers), and the Grammy winner Shabba Ranks.

But the competition is always fierce; in the time following the period covered by this book, it appeared for a while that the King's reign was seriously threatened, noticeably so after the senseless murder of King Tubby in 1989. Producers like the aforementioned Steely and Clevie, Bobby Digital, as well as Donovan Germain and a revitalised Sly Dunbar, began to make inroads into Jammy's dominance in the early 90s. In 1991 he silenced those critics who said he was finished with Pinchers' 'Bandolero', a huge hit that inspired many versions; this success was further underlined with the inexorable rise of the brilliant Bounty Killer, who had first been recorded by Jammy's brother Trevor in 1990, and went on to make three massive albums with Jammy's family (including Trevor and Jammy's son, John John). Along with Beenie Man, his great rival, Bounty Killer ruled the mid-90s dancehall, eventually setting up his own label in 1995 and embarking on a series of recordings that encompassed hardcore dancehall and collaborations with some of the leading lights of U.S. hip-hop. Bounty Killer also brought the new phenomenon of dancehall 'crews' into the music, starting off with his own Scare Dem Crew. But it was the hugely successful Ward 21 crew that revitalised King Jammy's once again with 'Haters', the dancehall tune of 1999, followed by the equally successful 'Bada Bada' and 'Bellyas'. Current dancehall ruler Elephant Man also got his start with Jammy's and his successes in 2001–2 testify convincingly to the durability of the King. That longevity looks guaranteed with the involvement of Jammy's sons, John John and Lloyd James Junior ('Jam II' in Beth's book). Both are successful producers, with their labels John John, Father & Son, and John Dog, and Jammy's brother Trevor continues with his Uncle T imprint.

I was pleased to be asked to contribute an afterword to this re-issue of Beth Lesser's *King Jammy's*. I can still recall the sheer enjoyment of reading Beth's book for the first time. It seemed to me then that nobody – with the honourable exception of the late Tero Kaski's excellent book on Henry 'Junjo' Lawes – had managed to 'get inside' the music to such a degree. Beth tells it like it is without romanticising, without adopting a false style, in clear-sighted and accurate prose; she is also one of the best reggae photographers. Her impressions were confirmed when I first visited Jamaica myself in 1991. Much that I saw then in Kingston – and Waterhouse in particular – was almost exactly as Beth had described it, in both its appearance and its inner workings. You can't ask for anything more than that; now let *King Jammy's* gain the new readership it surely deserves.

Steve Barrow
London, February 2002

Appendix

Selections from Reggae Quarterly

**Jammy's truck
in Waterhouse**

Greetings from Half Pint

Half Pint

When we last heard from Half Pint he had just
released an LP with Jammy entitled *Money Man
Skank* and had a brand new 45 called 'Winsome'.
Who could have guessed then that the song would
become such a massive hit. When 'Winsome'
played at a dance, all the girls would raise their
hands in the air and start to move. No other song
could satisfy people the same way. It became
a classic – a song that can be played anytime, any
year, because it just can't go stale.

That song was the real beginning of Pint's popularity.
Although his previous songs were just as good,
it was the Myrie and Marshall-produced 'Winsome'
that caught the public's attention. And Pint continued
to hold that attention by putting out one top song
after another without any filler material in between.
Soon after 'Winsome' came 'Political Fiction',
also on the Jammy's LP, which made an important
statement about the senselessness of politically-
based rivalries and war. And then came 'One in
a Million', produced by Jammy, which all but outdid
the success of 'Winsome'. The LP that featured
it was one of the most consistent, well-constructed
LPs in reggae. All the material is strong, and the
songs are well written. It included 'One Big Ghetto',
'You Lick Me First', 'Mr. Landlord', 'Puchilou', and
'What More Can I Really Do' – all songs that can sell
on their own as 45s.

Winsome

An odd thing happened with 'Winsome' though. Two years down the road, the Rolling Stones happened to hear it and became quite enchanted with it and desired the rights to record a cover version for their upcoming LP. As Pint explains, 'The first notion I had, it was the Rolling Stones' lawyer called Prince Jammy. He put me unto the number for the lawyer and in turn I make my lawyer call him and the business deal was set. Dynamic Sounds was the one they called first as one of the biggest distributors in the Caribbean [and the distributor for the album]. Then Eddie Lee contact Jammy and Jammy gave me the information. The lawyer told me they got the album out of a record shop and they were playing it – Jimmy Cliff and Mick Jagger himself and a couple more – in Europe or England – and they were doing some reggae tracks too.'

Once the business deal was complete, the Stones did their own version, re-titled 'Too Bad', and included it on their *Dirty Ways* LP with credit (and royalties) going to Pint.

Continuing his success with Myrie and Marshall, Pint recorded 'Hold On', an irresistible song that was released on a disco by Channel One in New York, and then 'Crazy Girl', his answer to the flood of 'Stalag' rhythm re-cuts. 'Crazy Girl' featured something new – Pint singing with a new spirit, more forceful and confident, even aggressive. The song explains what happened in the end with Winsome – she ran off – so perhaps the bitterness of the experience gave Pint's vocal abilities a new edge. Whatever the cause, Pint was suddenly sounding a lot more powerful, a sound he has continued to exploit in his subsequent releases.

It was in late 1984 that Pint began working with Sly and Robbie, a pair of musicians who only work with those whom they believe really have the talent to reach the masses of people outside Jamaica. 'Cost of Living' and 'Nightlife Lady' didn't come out until June of '86, but they are the first two songs released from an upcoming full LP. 'Cost of Living' features Sly trying out still another innovative drum pattern in which he has almost turned the beat backwards. Then came plans for the big Sly and Robbie tour – the rhythm twins with several of the acts they have worked with: Yellowman, Ini Kamoze, and Half Pint. The tour started in Miami in September, travelled north as far as Toronto, headed for the west coast, and then left for Europe and Scandinavia and eventually, the Far East.

On the first leg of the tour, they were accompanied by George Phang, the Powerhouse producer himself, the man responsible for Pint's biggest hit to date, 'Greetings'. 'Greetings I bring from Jah. To all raggamuffin', Pint sings, over still another new drum pattern from Sly. In combination with this driving, pounding beat, Pint's new Rambo-style delivery made 'Greetings' into (as Barry G claims) the new Jamaican national anthem. It was number one in the charts in Jamaica right up until the end of August when Mallory Williams knocked it off with 'She Boom'.

'Greetings'

'Greetings' was actually voiced in England and first released by Jetstar. Only afterwards did Sonic release it in Jamaica. It entered the British national charts briefly at number seventy-five and then disappeared. But that didn't stop people from buying it. It appealed to people because of the message, a message of support to the sufferers. And having emerged only recently from a life growing up in the heart of the ghetto, it's a message Pint is very sincere in sending. 'You have to remember: everybody's life value very much. And raggamuffin is not too much of a classy person who can afford to have on silk. But people like them, you have to look out for them and respect them, let them know them are worthwhile. Cause you can't turn your back on anyone.' So although Half Pint no longer lives in the slum, he still sends his greetings to all who remain and all who supported him while he was just a young singer trying a thing.

Beth Lesser
Reggae Quarterly 1, No. 7 (1986)

George Phang –
Powerhouse Producer

George Phang
relaxing at home

Right now, George Phang is big in the business. He's the fastest rising producer on the scene. His name is already made as a hit-maker and his productions are known internationally. He is respected in all countries that have been reached by reggae music. Quite a quick rise for a man who, up until a couple of years ago, wasn't really involved in music at all – except as an avid fan.

George has always had the music business in his blood. Even when he wasn't officially involved, he worked hard to boost certain young artists who needed a push. These artists have now come back to work with him and give him their best. People like Little John acknowledge George as the man who gave them their first big boost. From Little John, George got two big hits, 'True Confessions' and 'Roots Girl', two of the biggest dancehall tunes of 1983.

But that was only the beginning of George Phang's hit-making career. That same year he released Sugar Minott's 'Buy Off the Bar' and then Barrington Levy's 'Money Move', which went straight onto the charts without even bubbling underneath. The biggest song of the summer of 1984 has been George's 'Lick Shot' by Michael Palmer, a re-done version of a song Palmer originally cut at Channel One for the Tasha label. But only the lyrics are the same. The new rhythm made it another instant dancehall classic. The secret of George's success has a lot to do with Sly and Robbie, who play their very best on all George's productions. Both are close friends of his and have urged him from the start to begin a career in music.

How did you get involved in music?

It happen one day when me and Robbie [Shakespeare] end up somewhere, we deh de resting weself a way, where he say, 'Bwoy, it better the I deal with music, seen?' And I show him say, 'Yeah, we can go ina it.' It happen that me and him go a studio one Sunday and we deh a studio with Sly and Robbie, Willie Lyndo, and Dean Frazer them, and it's like, we lay a rhythm, the original called 'Soldier Man Rock'. Well, them say like he will give me a run off a it. So me say, 'Alright, better we just sit in and deal with a live session.' And we just sit in and we do a live session that day. And it's like me have the artists them all the while so him say, 'Boy, go ina it.' And me hear what him say and me just go ina it. Really them man a draw me in the record business, Sly and Robbie.

You already had known Robbie for a long time?

A long time – before me even start deal with record. We a move from long, long time – from youthman days. Be me did involve in something else. But me say, 'Alright, me just involve ina this – recording.' And, it's like me just go ina it and me really love it. The people them take on to my record.

What came out of your first session?

The session, we come out with a tune named 'Tribulation' with Eek-a-Mouse. Well, it never really reach nowhere too tough still cause it's like he did a do that record already for somebody – I believe it was Junjo he do it for – and then him come back again and do it for me. Junjo never really put out fe him own yet, but... Me no really too like a man do a thing and come back and do it for me. So, from me find that out, me just draw back that record.

Is the Powerhouse label only for your own productions?

Really, it's them [Sly and Robbie] and them hand it over to me to use it.

Did Clive Jarrett use it?

When him first started recording, he use it. It's my label now.

What was your first real hit?

My first hit really was the tune 'True Confessions' with Little John. It's like from there, so now me really put out more interest and say well – cause all the while it's like me never strongly deal with it – like me having one foot in and one foot out.

What gave you the idea to do-over that song?

One Sunday me a do some work and me a voice Little John and thing and me hear him sing that tune there, 'True Confession'. But him sing like the original ['Mr. Editor' by the Silvertones]. So we say, 'Yeah, we can use one or two lyrics from the original but we don't want exactly the original.' So it's like me kinda try it out – me and Archie [from Gemini Hi-Fi] and we say, 'alright', and Little John put in some little dancehall slur. We just do it that way there and we find out say it right! Cause everyone did love that tune there. When it burst is like even himself [Little John] get shock cause he never know say really it would make him more upstanding than him really was. Cause that music sell a whole heap. People still love it.

What made you decide to record Little John?

Well, from Little John is a youth, me is a man who always boost Little John. That was before me start deal with music. The first stage show him go pon really, Trench Town school, when the school did have a concert itself, it's like me go and get Little John now – them time he used to spar with a youth name Sour – so, like him and Sour come in, cause Sour did deejay and sing and it's like me say, 'Put Little John on the stage' and them say 'No.' And I say, 'Yeah, man, give him a break.' And him go pon the stage and it's like them come on it, seen? So from there so, really me a say well, this youth really can be a champion.

What about Barrington Levy?

Barrington Levy is a next one I have from a long, long time before him even start record. He even used to live in my house. All them time me never involve in the recording business. Till one day he said, 'Me a go do some recording for you.' Me say, 'No, me na too in the recording business.' Me and him, carry him go enough dance, and sing till Junjo first [artists]. The two of them help out one another.

You seem to have close relationships with your artists.

We grew up together in the ghetto and we know what is ghetto runnings. We kind stick to each other like one family still. Cause when you ina the music business, you have fe tell the whole of we are family.

How did you get the idea for the song 'Money Move'?

'Money Move'. Now, me and Barrington Levy drove one day and like we deh a one little garage and we listen to Jah Thomas' 'Shoulder Move', seen. So we can come up with something. We know our move supposed to be the right move, and the right move a money move. And we just come up with the idea and Barrington say, 'Yeah, man!' and him just say, 'Alright give me a couple days pon it and thing and let me see if we can hook up this thing right away.' It work out that we go a studio first time and it's like it never too sound too right, seen, when we a do it. Have fe just come back. We do some different recording until we get it now the right way, cause it did want more lyrics and we go ina it and just do it the right way.

You double-tracked his vocals on that.

You see, the harmonising business now, it's good when a man can harmonise like Sugar Minott cause Sugar Minott do him own harmonising. With the double-track now, we wouldn't call that harmonise still cause he just sing it straight. Only thing we do is build up one voice and draw down one voice.

'Buy Off the Bar' with Sugar Minott was a big hit for you.

That's really say like this music is one in a million. Cause the lyrics was so put together. And every jukebox you go ina yard, it de deh. And before a man even start drink he say, 'buy off the bar.'

Do you think your production is changing the sound of music?

It already change. Cause if you notice my music whe you hear out there right now even sound different. Cause the musician them whe me a use, a them man a definitely change the sound of music.

You always use Sly and Robbie?

I have them two man there as the best right now,
seen. A them find the right rhythm. Really, of a fact,
Robbie really find certain baseline and say, 'Boy,
Phang, make we use this one.' And you'd a hear all
Robbie down ina the corner... and we just go ina it.

**The album you have with Charlie Chaplin has
a really new sound.**

You have a clap you put in front and me say the
clap stand up strong ina the rhythm all the while.
So you have to change it ca it don't make no sense
to hear one set of music all the while. Ca only
one instrumental hit you have, 'Unmetered Taxi',
and every producer, including myself too, a do
vocal, and we na really think fe do an instrumental
and it's Sly and Robbie that really come with it.

**Have you ever thought of starting your own
sound system?**

Well, me could afford it now. Me wouldn't say really
deal with a sound, call it my sound. Me woulda
more give a man ina the ghetto and say, 'Boy, a fe
your sound there ca me have a business. You gwan
and eat food offa that.' Ca you want too much thing
like – know a tune where Charlie Chaplin a say,
'What it pay a man to gain the world and loose his
soul.' And I no really see myself in that position.

Youth Promotion

Jah Stitch and Blacka T in front of the Youth Promotion truck

Just down Robert Crescent – downtown Kingston – stands the headquarters for Sugar Minott's Youth Promotion organisation. The front room, with the walls lined with posters and the paint peeled off where taped-up pictures were removed, constitutes the studio with voicing facilities next door in the master bedroom. Across the narrow hall, a group of children are doing their homework, and out back in the yard are congregating some of Jamaica's most talented youth. They are learning the music business directly from one of Jamaica's most experienced singers, the 'Godfather', Sugar Minott.

Sugar has come through sixteen years in the business to become one of reggae's best-loved entertainers at home and abroad. He has toured North America, Europe, and even Japan, attracting huge audiences everywhere. Sugar rose from ghetto youth to international superstar. But unlike many others in the same position, Sugar has chosen to put back into the music what he has reaped from it by adopting and teaching the talented youths in the ghetto, the real roots of reggae music.

'It's coming like Sugar is godsend.' That is something you will hear many Youth Promotion members say. Sugar is using his knowledge, contacts, and experience to give the youths some exposure and a fair break, to keep them from having to suffer the ripoffs and piracy he and many others of his generation had to go through.

Inside the Studio, Ken Minott, Sugar's little brother, is mixing a Youth Promotion special to be played by the sound exclusively. Al Campbell is in the bedroom with the headphones on voicing 'Gone Computerise' over Sugar's latest 'computerised' rhythm track. Out on the street, Knobby (also known as L. Wiggin) is loading the Youth Promotion car with records to carry around to all the record shops. Knobby, who serves as co-producer along with Sugar, also looks after getting stampers made, promotion, and other business affairs.

Back in the house, one of Sugar's many brothers or cousins is carefully preparing vegetables in a big pot over an open fire for the ital feast. Sugar is last seen driving up the road on a bicycle only to return an hour later with lots of the good, good sensi – enough for everyone. Soon the telephone chalice emerges and Bingi Gene disappears in a cloud of smoke.

Sugar Has Never Left His Roots

Sugar is a rarity in reggae today. He is one of the few singers to become a success internationally but never to forget his roots. His life began as a sufferer in the ghetto and he has never stopped singing about the hardships and realities of that life. His albums bear titles like *Ghettology* and *Sufferer's Choice* and his hits include tales of having to sell ganja to live ('Oh Mr. D. C.'), unemployment ('No Vacancy'), and just plain hard times ('Hard Time Rock'). From experience, Sugar knows that the talent of Jamaica is hidden away in its roughest ghettoes only awaiting an opportunity to express itself.

In 1979, Sugar began his first campaign to organise these talented youths into a group that could work together to secure their rights. His Black Roots label started out with singers like Tony Tuff, Tristan Palmer, Little John, and Barry Brown, all artists who are widely known and respected today. Tristan is even producing himself and others for the Black Solidarity label, while Little John owns his own Romantic sound system and label.

But due to the pressures at home, Sugar moved Black Roots to England and set it up overseas. For a time it worked well. Many of the artists (like Sandra Logan, Carol Thompson, and Musical Youth) rose to public acclaim on their own after getting a good start with Sugar. After a few years abroad, however, Sugar found his reputation changing, as he was becoming more and more identified with the 'lover's rock' style so popular in the U.K. So Sugar felt it was time to return to his roots. Once back in Jamaica, his first thoughts were of starting his collective all over again and getting Youth Promotion label 'back on top'.

'I'm trying to give the youths an opportunity that I never had,' Sugar explains, revealing the philosophy that drives the Youth Promotion organisation. 'For the youth in the ghetto, it's a pain to get even a simple thing like a shoes. And every Jamaican artist, you have to sing a series of free songs before you can make it. You have to just voice for everybody. We are trying to establish a place where you don't have to do that. You can come here to build up your talent and get your songs released through this organisation and, after a while, it's up to you what you want to do cause we can't help no big artist. After you reach a certain standard, it's up to you. Our company is designed just for newcomers.'

The Sound

While the Youth Promotion label offers new and
ready artists a first chance to test public reaction
by putting out a record, the Youth Promotion sound
system gives still more youths the opportunity
to develop their talents to the point where they too
can record. A few names associated with the sound
include: deejays Colourman, Blacka T, Daddy Ants,
Macka P, Dona P, and Jah Mikey, who are joined by
singers like Tenor Saw, Trevor Junior, little Yammy
Bolo, Lloyd Hemmings, and of course, Sugar himself,
who still sings live whenever the vibes strike him.
The selector now is Major Stitch, the deejay from
a few years back who was then known as Jah Stitch.
Jah Wise used to share the task but has since
departed for Washington to play the Emperor sound.
Tolousie does the mixing and Apachie puts the
records on the turntable; Sugar's brother, Pleasure
Minott, strings up the sound. Although the sound
was playing small dances and parties for a while, it
came on the road officially only in late 1984.

Jah Mikey

One of the main deejays for the sound, Jah Mikey,
has come from a long line of different sounds
to finally settle in with Promotion. Starting with
Emperor Faith in the days of Ranking Trevor and
U-Brown, Mikey has always been a popular live
performer, but has seldom been on record. He did
a few cuts for Joe Gibbs – the deejay parts that
followed another artist's vocals on disco – and had
a cut on Junjo's *Whole New Generation of Deejays*
LP. There was also a tune for Channel One, but, all
in all, it was not much of a recording career, though
his lyrics did make a hit record. Unfortunately,
it was for Smiley and Michigan, not for him. Mikey
originated the famous 'Nice Up the Dance' that
became such a huge success for the duo in 1979.
He even had put the song down on tape for producer
Tony Welch, but Welch wasn't sure that the lyrics
were 'ready' yet. So Coxsone Dodd beat him to it
and created one of the top 45s of the year.

Colourman

The other main deejay, Colourman, is a relative newcomer to the scene, though you wouldn't know it from the good following he's developed over a short time. Coming from Manchester, where he played with Cosmic Force, a country set, to Kingston in late 1984, Fidel Hugh Henry was discovered right away at a Gemini dance he was passing through. The next day he was with Promotion as an important part of the show.

Colourman has a distinctive voice and good, solid – though not flashy – lyrics. Most of his inspiration comes from the Bible, but he manages to make the good book sound like a party when he creates dancehall verse out of his story. And he does come up with some curious extras like: 'This is a question of style – special request to comma and apostrophe.' He's the only deejay yet to deliver dictionary definitions in the classic dancehall style.

So far, Colourman has his first 45, 'Skin it a Go Peel', (released by Youth Promotion) and a second on Connection, as well as a cut on the Channel One album of 'Adam and Eve' versions produced by the veteran deejay I-Roy.

Tenor Saw

What Youth Promotion specialises in is singers. The influence of Sugar Minott is felt when one hears the quality of the vocalists that the sound carries. These include Jamaica's 'little singer', twelve-year-old Yammy Bolo, who can be seen late into the night with the mike in one hand and a bottle of Heineken in the other.

Fast becoming the new 1985 sensation must be singer Tenor Saw, whose style and voice imitate no man. His first 45 was 'The Roll is Called' for George Phang's Powerhouse label. Gospel and dancehall met over a Sly and Robbie update of 'Queen Majesty' and made the song a dance favourite. But his next 45, 'Pumpkin Belly', Jammy's second cut to be released on his original 'Sleng Teng' rhythm, made Tenor Saw almost a hero. Keeping up his reputation for essential dancehall cuts, Tenor Saw followed up with 'Ring the Alarm' for Techniques. 'Ring the alarm, another sound is dying.' The song has been put to good use in many sound clashes. Meanwhile, Youth Promotion released 'Pumpkin Belly II', their own version of 'Lots of Sign'.

Saw sings directly from his own experience, which gives his lyrics a personal flavour. He tells the story of what inspired him to write the song 'Pumpkin Belly': 'When I was small and at home, my mother used to say, "Stay inside – don't leave the yard." And when she turn her back – leave and gone with some friends, [I] run around and play some games. When I get back, probably, my mother isn't home so Granny say, whenever I do something wrong, "You know how water walk go a pumpkin belly, hear boy?" She was always saying that, whenever I do something wrong. And not her alone. I hear other people in her age bracket say the same thing. After a long while, I didn't hear it no more so I say, alright, I'm going to sing it a bring it back.'

Saw's first LP is to be released on Youth Promotion, but Saw really wants to do all his own work for himself alone – everything from laying the rhythms to getting the discs pressed. 'I've been watching his business for a long time. Everything Sugar does, I watch. So I know how it works.' Tenor Saw is a youth with a lot of ambition and enough talent to make his mark on the music.

But the show wouldn't be complete without Promotion's own 'lickshot', Jackie Knockshot. The style was originated by the one Joe Lickshot who started out vocalising gun noises and later advanced to recreate the sounds of bombs and tear gas. Jackie has expanded his own repertoire of 'shots' to cover Japanese sword clashes and even a beef patty race. His first appearance on record is on Sugar Minott's 'War and Crime', released on Youth Promotion.

Credit too must be given to selector Major Stitch, a man with a real history in the reggae business. If you remember songs like 'Greedy Girl', 'Marshall Dread', and 'Dread Can't Dead', you'll recall the deejay Jah Stitch who seemed to disappear from the scene a while back. In fact, Stitch only stopped deejaying live. He now selects and often operates the sound and is currently working on an LP for himself. The songs on the LP will all still reflect his classic style and deal with the same topics of reality that Stitch is known for. 'Man like we – me and Big Youth – our music have fe stand because the things we talk about never stop. Cause first time my music was about death, wickedness. Them things never stop. Dancing music, I like the music but I don't like the deejay style. They don't really say something. I do a tune like say "Dread Can't Dead" – it's something that happen to me cause me get shot and me survive and come back in the studio. So me like tune with meaning. Me like the music cause the music will always live. The music keep the people alive.'

At Youth Promotion, the music is keeping many youths alive and giving them a chance to explore and develop their individual talents. It's also a place they can get regular work playing with the sound until they are able to record. A lot of youths would have nowhere to turn if it weren't for the music. A whole generation of creativity would be lost to poverty.

Stitch remembers when he first started to get involved in music. At that time he was singing before he began to deejay. Men like the Heptones, Roy Shirley, the Wailers, Carlton and the Shoes, used to gather together in one big yard, a 'music yard'. 'One man with a guitar just a play until everybody just join in. Thirty people there and all thirty are musicians. Even Carl Dawkins, Stranger Cole... All singers. You hear one man just take note, take a lead, and when him done the next man just take it.'

In this way, the major talents of the past decade of reggae were developed, in one big 'music yard' in the ghetto. The same process is taking place everyday in Sugar's yard with Sugar serving as father, teacher, employer, and adviser to tomorrow's stars. To these youths, Sugar, 'The Godfather', stands for what an impoverished youth from the ghetto can achieve with just his talent and determination.

Sugar's long-time dream was to build up a sound. Now that he has accomplished this goal so well, he is working on making the Youth Promotion house into a real, official studio, complete with facilities to make rhythms, voice, and mix. Sugar enjoys bringing new artists into the public eye and, with his ear for talent and knowledge of the music business, his organisation will surely be seen in years to come as another Studio One, a 'university' of music where the best got their first lessons. But, for now, Sugar is struggling to keep the sound and label running. With a lot of hope, inspiration, and talent he's working to keep Youth Promotion going strong.

The Croaking Lizard:
Prince Jazzbo

Prince Jazzbo

Prince Jazzbo has been a deejay, producer, and general supporter of reggae music for over ten years. With an incredible enthusiasm for all aspects of the music business, Jazzbo (Linval Carty) stays very active but prefers to function on his own, out of the limelight. Jazzbo's work as a deejay has become as legendary as it is colourful. First, the Studio One days: 'Jah Dreader Than Dread', 'School', and 'Crabwalking' to name only a few. And of course, the recording feud between he and I-Roy, another popular deejay of the day. First to Jazzbo's head, then back to I-Roy's head. Lyrics constantly flung back and forth in a competitive but good-natured manner with no official winner declared. That was left to the record-buying public to decide.

And one can't forget Prince Jazzbo's classic LP, *Natty Passing Through Rome*, issued in the U.S. as *Ital Corner*. His apocalyptic lyrics and 'dreader than dread' delivery, coupled with producer Lee Perry's haunting rhythms, made this LP historic – the 'croaking lizard' at his best. The man who said 'step forward youth' on record for Bunny Lee, did just that. Back in the mid-seventies, Jazzbo was one of the first deejays, if not the first, to produce his own material. Now a producer, he works with developing young artists like singers Horace Ferguson and Patrick Andy, as well as getting good work out of seasoned veterans like Horace Andy and Hugh Griffiths. With experience and optimism as his guide, Jazzbo will be creating a lot of music over the next few years including a full LP of his own material.

As Prince Jazzbo himself once said, 'Two steps forward, not steps backward.' And when Prince Jazzbo talks, you would be foolish not to listen.

How did you get your start working with a sound system?

Well, when I was around seven, I realised that my uncle had two sound systems. I start to move around. I wasn't really perfect then. I never really think of making a career of it when I start. I was just for pleasure. Days like those, the music wasn't on such a large scale like now. No one used to think of export or import or foreign sales. No one would even think to come interview a deejay. It took you thirteen years to come interview me. In 1967 I start to deejay disco in Spanish Town.

When did you begin to take your career seriously?

Well, funny enough, the serious part of the business came when I start to hear my records on the radio. I hear it at dances, at parties, write up in the paper, etc. Then I think, more or less, I'm doing a great job.

How did you feel about your getting famous?

I felt great about it but then a lot of popularity and less funds, lots of commitments you cannot really afford. So, you find you get a big popularity, you get quite famous, but you really cannot live up to the standard of the popularity because it means money.

You fist recorded for Coxsone Dodd. How did he find you?

He came to me one night. It was the December 31. We had a competition in Spanish Town. Our sound was the smallest sound and we had a competition with the biggest sound named Ruddy's. It was deejay by I-Roy and my sound, named Whip, was played by Whip, selected by Whip, and disc jockey by Prince Jazzbo. We had a great fight that night. It end up that I win the contest and Coxsone Dodd say that I must come to the studio the next morning. I was so glad I never really remember to ask him where the studio was. I ask someone else and I get the information and I went there. I never get to record that morning. It was a Saturday morning and I went the Sunday again and did the 'Door Peep'. I think that was the hardest rhythm in Coxsone's studio. Those times he was looking for a deejay who could compete with Big Youth, U-Roy, Dennis Alcapone. He was looking for someone who could sell. Cause he always wanted to be a champion in the business.

How was your relationship with Mr. Dodd?

Me, I couldn't give **Coxsone** no bad name. **Cause
if there was no Coxsone, there would be no reggae
music. I** would like to give **Coxsone** more praises
every day – long life and good health and strength.
He's a very nice man to deal with, to talk to. He's
quite clever. To me, **Coxsone** is one of the best ina
the business cause **Coxsone** have 200 artists and
musicians, and grow up acts in the business and no
producer do like **Coxsone** do. **Cause** like now, it's
more modern, more scientific, more brain-strain. **So,**
now a man will give you $200 and you don't see him
for two years. **But** in **Coxsone** days, every singer
or musician could go to **Coxsone** and get a $10 or
a $20 or some records to go sell.

I never stop working with **Coxsone. Coxsone** is the
only man I will always do tune for, anytime **Coxsone**
want me. I don't record for any man but myself and
Coxsone is the only man. **Him** na have fe give me
money. **Him** na have fe tell me to come record. **All**
me have fe do is tell him, 'What happen Mr. Dodd?
I would like to do a tune,' and him say, 'Yeah, man.
Come.' Some of my best is on **Studio One. He is**
a producer, also a good arranger. **Coxsone** always
wants a singer or a musician to put out what
Coxsone wants and he have a very good capability
of listening. **And** through that, more singers always
got their best recording done at **Studio One.**
Coxsone have the idea, he have a studio – you can
go to **Coxsone** every day and work pon one tune.
If it no right, him na want it. **Him,** na say, 'Yes, it's
good.' **Him** listen to every bar, everything, before
him pass it. **So** him always get good work.

When did you decide to start producing?

As I say before, making me popular was just
popularity. So I think more or less, being popular –
it was Glen Brown who influence me, give me
$175 to voice a tune, 'Mr. Harry Skank'. Then him
make a money and him encourage me. Him say,
'Watchaman, look into the future. If you start now
to walk with your bag and sell your tune yourself,
you're better off.' He said to me, 'Listen Jazzbo,
I will give you a rhythm but you have to voice
two tune' and him give me a rhythm and the rhythm
was a tune named 'Mr. Wanton', the rhythm I do
'Concubine' on. After I do 'Concubine', it make a
good start. Ever since that tune, I can always make
a tune.

**Wasn't it hard to get the funds to produce
independently?**

In the early days things wasn't so difficult like now.
Things was more cheaper. You get more people who
want to help out people.

You also worked with Lee Perry.

Yeah, I done some album for Lee Perry, about
thirteen tune: 'Penny Reel', 'Croaking Lizard', 'Natty
Pass Through Rome'. I get $1,000 advance.

Brad's in New York pressed the LP *Ital Corner*?

Yeah, but Brad's dead. Who's gonna pay now?

How did the feud with I-Roy get started?

Well, that was started by nature. I, I-Roy, Bunny Lee – we were at [King] Tubby's studio one night. I-Roy went in to voice a tune, this tune that name 'Straight to Jazzbo Head'. We were always driving each other from youth days cause we were from the same town and I popular in my town more than him. So, I-Roy went in to voice the tune and started driving, man! Drive, drive, drive – until (I never like it) it sound nice but I never like it. Tubby's was recording it. Then Tubby say, 'Boy, it nice, you know.' Bunny Lee start laugh. Anyway, they send me to do one tune but me never do it. About three weeks later, I-Roy one start sell so the competition get hot now. Then me answer him with 'Straight to I-Roy Head', a Bunny Lee production too. Anyway, it wouldn't stop him. He did a whole heap to Jazzbo head. I do next one and just done. You see, the work I do, I no really ina no form of negative work. I woulds like to say something positive all the time so a youth twenty or fifteen years younger than I can learn something from it.

You lived abroad for a time.

In 1976 I spent three years in London. I never liked London. So, I run away from London – just leave London for three weeks' holiday in Jamaica and I leave my house, my missus, my kids, my clothes, everything in London. When my three weeks was up, I think more: No place like home and three weeks is too short. So I think like tearing up the ticket. And that's what I did. Since then, a lot of times I felt like go, but when the time got ready I left like stay because this world is not only for money.

Most producers do a lot of travelling to sell their product.

I want to stay in Jamaica. Jamaica is a farm, you know, like American is a market. I don't think you have to go a market to sell my food. I would like to stay on the farm and buy it, ship it, to America or England to sell.

You did an album called *Soca Rockers* that was a bit different from your other work.

I don't really like that tune, you know. I think it was one of my worst tune. Because, why I say it was one of my worst tune: After I finish with work, I get to understand the tune was against my work. Cause soaking the rockers – cause roots rock reggae I make – and Soca Rockers, that mean it's soaking up the rockers. But then it come like I have to do that record. I won't explain why. If any of my fans hear that record and doesn't like it, they could forgive me still.

Do you deejay with any sound now?

Yeah, but the way I work sound now is quite different from the younger days. See, in the western part of Jamaica, most sound owners depend on me for most of the music. Now, I am one of the oldest and youngest producers in the business. So sound men know I know every man in the business: who made the most music, what year an artist fly out. People in the western part of Jamaica depend on me for music weekly. At the moment I'm responsible for eighteen sound in Jamaica. At the moment there's a sound in Spanish Town by the name of Creation. I'm the one who build it. I'm the road manager for it. Kung-Fu (the selector), Michigan and Smiley, Branniff, Flatty deejays most nights. They gang me up, lift me up, bus two lyrics and things. Me always have the baddest lyrics to draw.

How did you get the name Brisco for your label?

Brisco is my family name, the name of my mother and grandmother who grow me up. And the two dogs [on the label] represent the society that they was living into. They were more a churchical and sophisticated type of life.

What about your new label, Ujama?

Ujama is not my new label. Prince Jazzbo is my new label. The name Ujama is a form of self-help. The amount of figures that make up the name Ujama, they represent people – four lawyers and myself. When I was living in the U.K. we had a get together to do some business, to build a recording company, and we use a letter from each of us name. We fix it to get Ujama. The donkey on it is part of humbleness. I'm riding, if you notice, it's me and a princess on it, riding to Africa.

Have you ever been to Africa?

I don't really tell people them thing there cause me is a dread now and always seek for repatriation. I always thinking of repatriation to Africa because I know is where I belong. I can't really stay in Babylon for the rest of my life because I see Jamaica is Babylon, all the Western hemisphere is Babylon. So, I can't stay in Babylon forever, just live and dead. I would like to go somewhere to live for live.

It seems like you put a lot of thought into everything you do, from your labels to your music.

If you is a king, anything you are doing, you have to make sure you are doing it positive, like you have a future in what you are doing. In fifty years to come you have to have a proper reason why you started doing what you did.

King Jammy

**Johnny Osborne
across the street
from Jammy's yard**

On 23 February 1985, Jammy's Hi-Power exploded on the scene with 10,000 watts of pure sound, a crew of Waterhouse's hottest entertainers, and a brand new pre-release rhythm with a sound that could change the course of reggae – the computerised 'Sleng Teng'.

Around 1980, Jammy's disco had been going strong. But time and changes in Jammy's workload allowed the set to fade into oblivion, leaving the gap in Waterhouse to be filled by Black Scorpio. Even when Jammy's was playing, entertainers in the area would split their time between both sets, going with whoever was playing that night.

But on 23 February, the artists had to take sides. Scorpio carried the two horsemen, Sassafras and General Trees, along with Shuka Shine, singers Wayne Palmer, Culture Lee, Michael Jahson, and some killer dubplates by Frankie Paul, Earl Sixteen, and Bobby Melody. Jammy had John Wayne, General Leon, Screecha Nice, singers Echo Minott and Wayne Smith, and an infinity of 'Sleng Teng' versions.

The yard was already filled with people by nine o'clock and more kept coming in. Scorpio started with some Little John on dub, building up to his classic 'Weather Balloon' update. Then it was Frankie Paul's 'The Closer I Get to You', then a few tunes by Johnny Osbourne, all of which led up to his Earl Sixteen selection, 'Sweet Soul Rocking' and 'Making Tacks'.

After an hour, Jammy's opened up with a 'Sleng Teng' pounding from the boxes and the crowd went wild, blowing noisemakers and cheering like New Year's Eve at midnight. It was a dramatic entrance for Jammy back into the sound business. Since that night Jammy has become so much in demand that most weekends are spent travelling out to various country destinations that are just waiting to see the return of the King.

Always in Touch

Even though Jammy wasn't playing his sound for a while, he never lost touch with the scene. He and Channel One shared most of the dubcutting work done on the Island and many specials were voiced in his cramped four-track studio.

Jammy began his engineering career as an apprentice to King Tubby in 1976. His electronics training was his recommendation and he began by mixing a lot of material coming out of the Dromily Avenue studio, before moving on to produce his own work for himself. But even with the producing and the travelling that came later, Jammy never left his sound.

Having started in the 1960s, it was playing throughout the late seventies with artists like Nicodemous, Errol Scorcher, and Kojak and Liza. Even when he lived in Toronto, Canada for six years, Jammy kept playing a far-north version at basements around the city while doing a little engineering with Jerry Brown at Summer Sounds studio. It was when he returned to Jamaica and got hooked up with King Tubby that the musical history of Jammy's begins.

How did you get started with Tubby?

Pat Kelly was engineering there. Phillip Smart was in New York, just left. I don't know why Tubby's really wanted me. I guess because we are coming from way back.

What were you working on those times?

It used to be mostly Yabby You stuff and Bunny Lee. Those were the two major producers that we used to work for in those days.

When did you start your own recording?

About 1977, just a year after I started. Other producers encouraged me. Yabby You was one of the first producers who encourage me. He even gave me the first rhythm. It was a tune name 'Born Free' with Black Uhuru. That was the first tune I make. It wasn't released in Jamaica. In those days they were releasing 7" reggae music in England so I went to England in 1977 at Christmas. We didn't give it any company. They didn't have any major reggae company apart from Island, so it was released by a guy named Fatman. We did it on our own. We drove around all about in England and in the country. It didn't do good. The group was new. No one knew them.

What other music did you have with you then?

I had some Cornell Campbell, a group named the Travellers – a couple of tunes with them – Hugh Black, the deejay [not the one with Joe Gibbs but the one before him].

What did you do when you came back?

That's when I did the Black Uhuru album [*Love Crisis*]. They had a different sound and I'm always interested in people with a new sound. If you notice, that's why I have more talent all the time: because I like to have a new sound. I like to have young artists. I like to bring them my way. If you keep recording the same artists – everybody that was coming from in the sixties – the music just going to sound the same way.

So the Black Uhuru was your first LP? What was the first song to appear on your label?

Remember that white-spotted label? I took a single off the LP, 'Natural Mystic'.

When did you leave Tubby's?

About three years ago, 1982. I didn't leave Tubby's outright. You see, Tubby wanted me to control the studio and he wouldn't have another engineer. But I think it was best to get somebody to assist me when I am not around. Because, I mean, Tubby wasn't giving me really a big money. So I had to go out and seek for myself. That's why I started producing more and going to England, because I met Mojo records and I started working close with Mojo.

How did you come to build your own studio?

I went to London and I saw some mixing boards and I bought one for about £200, the first one. I have it inside my house there. The first machine I got, I got from Black Joy [Records], a two-track machine. I swap him for a dub LP.

What about your sound?

I had my sound from in the 60s and again from about 1978. I was the greatest sound them times. Still the greatest sound but it wasn't on the road for a while. Me build the set. I build all those amplifier. More power. You see, the manufacturer only recommends certain power so me just go above that.

What happened to your set the last time you had it on the road?

What really happen is that it wasn't really owned all by me. It was a partnership between me and another guy and he wasn't acting fair on my behalf so I decided to be lackadaisical with it, don't really pay it much time, and it just started failing out. I knew that if it happened that way, and it just failed out, I could go on my own. But I didn't want to just say, 'Take my name off of it.' Probably he would feel, a way, hurt.

An old disco 45 you have with Junior Reid, 'Jail House' on Imperial, the back says 'The Crowning of King Jammy'.

I think that time was the time when they crown me King Jammy's. I think it was in that same period of time and my name was getting boosted in England that time so it mention me as King Jammy's now.

Was that your first record with Junior Reid?

I did about three tracks that same time. I have one of them now that is still not released and it sounding good.

On the *Jah Fire* LP, two of the tracks are Locksley Castell, not Hugh Mundell, aren't they?

Yeah, I didn't have a full LP with Hugh Mundell.

Why did you stop working with Black Uhuru?

They weren't pleased with the deal that I got.

When you first set up here you just had the two-track machine. When did you get the dubcutter?

Two years ago. We cut the cleanest dub. And the music too. We have more music than the rest of places that cut dub. Being as I produce music, what I do, I get a lot of artists to sing 'specials' just to cut on dub. Some of those tune will never release.

What was your first number one record in Jamaica?

'Sleng Teng'. Before that I never had a number one record in Jamaica. 'Water Pumpee' [Johnny Osbourne] was about number five.

What about England?

The first number one was a Sugar Minott tune, 'Never Too Young'.

You never had a number one in Jamaica before 'Sleng Teng'?

No, because I never used to release so much music in Jamaica. I was more directing my business to England, more money and thing, you know. For you to get a number one tune in Jamaica, you don't just get a number one tune like you do in England. You have to all know certain announcer, drop off some cash, and all them thing. England now, I prefer the record business in England. More organised.

Tell me about Digital Bobby?

Can't leave out Digital Bobby! My right-hand man that can't right now. Digital Bobby start from about a year ago. Him used to do technician work and I always know him as a devoted guy, devoted to him work. He is not a guy who love money. He would love to have a career in this business. So is that I like him for. Because I had to work hard to really reach the stage where I am now. Bobby is one of the quickest learning guy I ever met. He can do everything in there just like myself. Only if anything wrong with the board, anything major, I have to go inside.

Can he decide whether to voice a new singer?

What we do, we have auditions every Saturday
morning. So what Bobby really do: I explain to him
that if a singer can sing, if he sounds good, just
record him. Probably when we record him, we can
listen back his potential that he have on a tape.
So when we listen back, we can know how we can
work from there. We can write good tunes for him
to start sing if him don't have lyrics and train him.

**February 23 was the official re-opening of Jammy's
sound?**

What really happen, the type of music that I used to
play in the older days, five years ago or so, a lot of
those musics can still play now but because they
are not available, the other sound system men can't
get it to play. But we still have some of those tune.
The older people just keep on remembering those
days. And I am one of the only sound that bring out
bigger folks to dance nowadays, not just the youth
them alone.

It was a nice crowd there.

Those people follow me all the way from Waterhouse.
Them love me. And me love them too.

'A Me Name Tiger'

Tiger working on
his music at home

The big blue Tiger-mobile can be heard all the way down St. Lucia Road as it comes roaring up towards King Jammy's with Tiger's latest rhythms pounding from the speakers and a host of friends in the back dancing in place and eating patties. Out comes Tiger with a crisp video camera perched on his shoulder and proceeds to film his ramble through the studio, including the people, the walls, everything. The result is later to be viewed at home on his brand new video setup that includes more than one deck for dubbing movies. The Tiger mobile is ready to pull out again. It can be easily recognised by the license plate, Tiger 1, the windshield inscription, 'a me name Tiger', and the blaring music – all the latest from the roaring Tiger.

'When you write this, remember to tell the people I'm special. Cause I really am special.' Yes, Tiger really is special. He builds all his own rhythms on his front porch before a crowd of avid fans from all around the neighbourhood. First he brings out the Casio keyboard amp and places it across from his patio chair. On top of this goes the cassette dubbing deck. To top it off comes the Tascam four-track mixing board. When all the proper electrical connections have been made and the cords pulled to one side, Tiger brings out the Roland 505 drum machine and sets a bass drum pattern. With the bass drum going, he plays with the switches, first adding timbale, then claps, and finally rim shot. When the audience starts visibly moving to the beat, Tiger knows he's hit the right pattern and leaves it beating away while he goes for one of his several Casio keyboards. This he places across his lap and begins to punch out a one-finger bass line. Soon, Tiger is in a world of his own, bopping away to the ever-changing melody, improvising freely on the beat.

'I can do something that no deejay ever do yet – build him own rhythm. You know seh you have deejay up there a see that. You can't stop them from vex cause it ina them fe vex about certain things. Like "Tiger really have a margin over we, you know. Imagine! The man build him own rhythm." Well, I come fe kill!'

Many of the rhythms on the RAS LP, *A Me Name Tiger*, and the Kangol clash LP between Tiger and Yellowman, were built by Tiger. From where does his inspiration for unusual rhythms (like the one on 'Lyrics for Your Money') come? 'You know where I got that offa? You know that cartoon where you see the man them a dance but them can't dance? [sings off key]: I'm sitting on a railroad. Some little funny dance? You see cartoon? God bless cartoon! Cause cartoon make me gwan them way there you know. Comic strip. When you get the Friday *Star*, the cartoon page – a that me wan see first. Yeah man! Sunday magazine – let me see the cartoon page.'

But cartoons alone are not responsible for the sounds and lyrics that flow out of Tiger. His next great inspiration is the world of old time comedy films like those starring the Marx Brothers and the Three Stooges. Inside the house, the same video machine can play movie after movie of all the old greats. The machine is stacked several feet high, with movies to be called upon at any time for inspiration or enlightenment.

Tiger, himself, has proven to be an inspiration to much controversy. In the *Sunday Gleaner*, the Reverend Clinton Chislome declared in print that 'any society in which Tiger's record "Wanga Gut" can make a number one position on the pop chart must be a sick society.' Never has a song been so universally misunderstood since 'One Love Jamdown' in 1980. Had no one even bothered to listen to the lyrics? The song was held back from airplay for a long time on the pretext that they thought it contained derogatory remarks about pregnant women. Luckily someone did listen to the song. Oddly enough, that someone was a noted political correspondent for the *Gleaner*, Carl Wint. He came to Tiger's rescue in a very comprehensive article in the *Sunday Gleaner* on January 30, 1987, to which the headline reads: 'Wanga Gut is Almost Like a Scripture.' Mr. Wint went on to speak of Tiger's intentions in glowing terms and to include the entire lyrics to the song for general inspection. He added: 'What he [Tiger] is enjoining fellow citizens to do is work hard, to eschew greed and avarice and envy' and suggested that an 'apology is due to Tiger.'

Tiger's response to the reverend gentleman? 'That man is impertinent!' Who can really criticise Tiger's lyrics? Not one of his songs defends slackness, drugs, or violence. His themes are instructional, humorous, and patriotic. 'Na Lef Ya' expresses his sentiments about always wanting to return to Jamaica no matter where his travels bring him while working. 'Me coulda gone a foreign the first time and stay – turn millionaire. Boy, me and the man them, immigration! The boy there a say 'How come you get three days and is all half a day and you wan come home?' I tell you if them have a place that coulda take me home after the show done, me woulda come home.'

Tiger's lyrics are also humourous. 'Come, Patty Page, make we dance pon stage,' he sings, adding, 'She can't sure me. It's like my lyrics: Come Chaka Khan, come dance with the don. Maybe it will give her a boost. She will ask, "What are they saying about me?" And they will have to tell her that "He is just saying he wants to dance with you."'

Starting out as a singer, Tiger made his first record, 'Why Can't You Leave the Dreadlocks Alone', for Phillip Grant in 1977. It was first released in Canada on a disco. He is also the same Tiger who sang 'Love Line' for Lloyd Campbell in 1982. Back then he was with a sound called Inner City Vibes before joining Black Star in 1985. During his Black Star time, he recorded 'Must Girlie Girlie', without response, and 'Puppy Love', which began to make his name known, as the whispers and rumours began spreading that Tiger had made the rhythm for that song all by himself. 'Wanga Gut' was Tiger's breakthrough song and his first number one. This was also the debut release on his orange and black Tiger label. Tiger's first LP was the clash with Yellowman on Kangol and it contained 'Don is Don' and 'Lyrics for the Money'. Then came 'A Me Name Tiger', released in the U.S. by RAS records and in England by Island. Follow up 45s have included the anti-drug 'Don't Paro' (i.e. don't get paranoid), 'Right Through the Gate', which was in support of dancehall deejays, and 'Daddy's Marcus', a contribution to the Marcus Garvery memorial that he made with Bagga Brown and the Jay's.

Tiger's love of music is rivalled only by his love of animals. His yard is slowly growing into a true jungle. Presently it is occupied by two puppies (Binner and Scubidoo), two hamsters, two parrots (Heckle and Jeckle), and some rabbits. Tiger is proud to display the additions he's made to his once-tiny house during the last year. One of these is the porch on which all of his rhythms are created. 'These rhythms now, a man will say, "Oh yes you build one," like him can't believe say a me. Wan come catch a me yard now! Anyone of those youth now, anything them a go crazy over, a that me come a road with first. Like "Don't Paro" – one hell when "Paro" done, you know.'

The name Tiger came from his father who was named Tiger before him. As a child he resented the name. Any boy who called him Tiger, he would block from coming through the lane. 'They had to go all the way around!' But later he began to like being called Tiger with all its connotations of a mighty beast. It was a name made to excite admiration and awe. Now that so much fame and attention has come to centre on him, Tiger finds being in the limelight both enjoyable and irritating. He laughs at the 'bicycle man' who runs straight into the 'walk-foot man' on the road because both are staring at him. But the girls who suddenly find qualities in him that they never saw before – 'Let me tell you a little part about that,' Tiger jumps in. 'How me so cute and me never did cute when me was small? You wan see the joke: All of the girls me used to know from my area, [I] see them a foreign: "You don't remember me through you get so big now? You no remember Annie?" A joke, seen?' And when he is away from home, 'It's always "Tiger come stay a me house. Though you a deejay now you must stay a me house." A whole heap of things you have to encounter.'

Tiger looks around to see who is smoking a cigarette. An ex-smoker himself, the very scent is offensive to him now. He now neither smokes nor drinks. At the moment he is upset about a promoter who has come from a big U.S. city and asked him to do a show and stay at a motel. 'Motel? Motel? I like to stay at the Holiday Inn.' His manager failed to spot this flaw in the plan and had the audacity to endorse it. This upsets Tiger greatly. It's hot and he's tired and in a terrible mood... until the music starts to play. Nothing can revive a person so fast. Soon, the motel, the cigarette, the manager are all forgotten as Tiger, grinning a true tiger grin from ear to ear, is picking out a melody on his keyboard and the fans are dancing around the house, and everything is alright again.

Beth Lesser
Reggae Quarterly 1, No. 8 (1987)

Admiral Bailey

Admiral Bailey

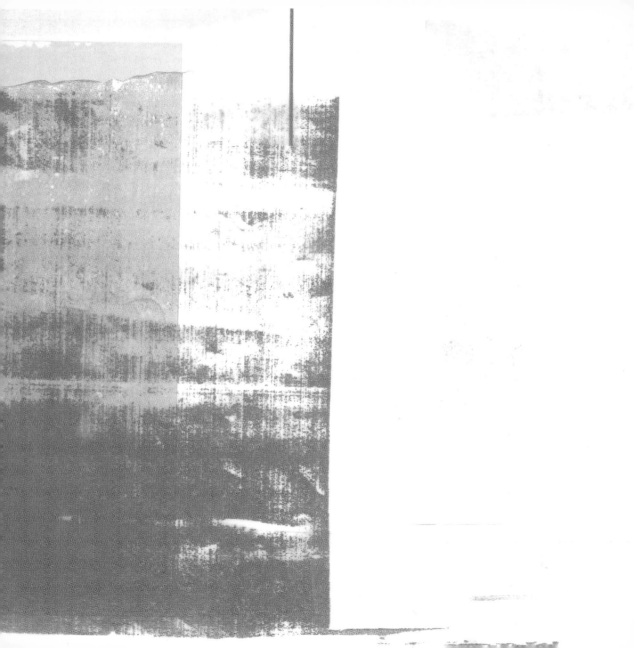

Admiral Bailey started life as a deejay 'a long time ago on the corner at Cockburn Penn.' He and his friends used to take in Stur-Gav with Ranking Joe and Jah Screw:

So, we used to go to dance and listen to Joe and come back on the corner and who can flash the most Ranking Joe lyrics win. Till one night we go to a wedding – a sound named Twilight. The brother gave me a talk on the sound and from that me start deejay pon him sound. One night a dance a keep at Tower Hill with Twilight and the owner for Metromedia was there. That time Peter Metro was in foreign and he asked me if I would like a job on his sound. Through I hear about Metromedia a long time, that was a big breakthrough for me. So I started to deejay on Metromedia and people get to like me and things. Well anyhow, through I was the last one to come on Metromedia and Metromedia was going to England, I didn't go. They leave me behind and that was a next setback there again. So I go back on Twilight until a next sound named Roots Melody like me and me de deh again, and from Roots Melody me really get to Jammy. Bobby Digital came out at Bay Farm Road and Olympic Way and the sound a play and him hear me deejay and come tell Jammy about me and Jammy call me and from deh so my career begins.

Bailey's career really does begin with Jammy's. Although he had previously made a record or two, since they received no airplay, Bailey feels he wasn't really recognised by the public as a deejay until he started putting out material for Jammy. 'No Stop Say So' made a little dent but the real boost came with 'One Scotch, One Bourbon' done with fellow Jammy's deejay Chakademus. The lyrics play off an old R&B tune by Amos Milburn that was a huge hit in Jamaica before Jamaica had a music of its own. 'The idea was Chakademus' – the topic of it. But each of our lyrics was our own. That tune bust us a lot. That tune let us get enough stage shows. It made us get twelve stage shows last year from that song.'

Controversial Lyrics

Bailey's reputation as 'Admiral Bailey who makes hits daily' as been built on some controversial music. With Josie Wales, Bailey made 'Ballot Box', a specific response to the rumours that were widely circulating that Josie and Bailey had been seen stealing a ballot box full of votes during the July 29, 1986 elections. 'The main purpose of that record was to set the record straight – make everybody know that is rumour. To set the record straight. "A who say the Colonel, a who say the Admiral thief the ballot box. Look how we big, look how we fat – how we fe jump fence with ballot box?" A joke man, a joke! Because right now me have my future ahead of me. Me can't bother mix up in the politics thing. I'm pleading for them don't brand me because politician never give me nothing. Everything I have, I have fe work for it.'

Likewise, 'Two Year Old' caused a controversy and was immediately banned from airplay on Jamaican radio. A universal misunderstanding arose as to what the lyrics really meant. Many thought it must be some kind of perversion to talk about a two-year-old child, little realising the age mentioned was that of a race horse fresh and ready to run, not a human. And as for the women who were offended by the reference to 'frowsy arms' etc., Bailey claims he is only telling girls that they must try to be clean and neat at any age.

But by far the most controversial of Bailey's tunes so far, and his biggest hit – in fact the main force in reggae for all of '87, was 'Punaany', another song too slack to be granted airplay on either of Jamaica's two radio stations. 'Punaany' still created such a commotion that two full LPs based on the 'Punaany' rhythm and theme followed quickly along with another avalanche of imitation and follow-up singles.

That song alone made Bailey the biggest sensation of the year and ensured that deejays would continue their precedence over singers for some time to come. And it also guaranteed that anything Bailey put on vinyl would hit. Like his follow up, 'Healthy Body', which utilised the same rhythm and format as 'Punaany' but said, 'Give me the Irish, give me potato' etc. – lyrics eminently more suitable for airplay. In fact, the success of 'Healthy Body' took even Admiral Bailey by surprise. 'The "Healthy Body" thing was made for radio purpose. I wasn't looking for that result. That just gave me inspiration fe go ina it and know me is dangerous!' Because to do back over a tune in that way – nuff people say me do 'Healthy Body' better than 'Punaany'.

But Bailey is made of more than slack lyrics. His 1987 releases are to include songs like 'Try Some Hustling', a song directed towards youth who 'pick up a gun'. Bailey explains: 'I want them to try some hustling, try some selling – anything, box juice, cigarette – just try some hustling.' There's also 'Head a Hurt Me', which tells of the people in his community who 'used to criticise me and say "gwan look work." Now I get some ambition and make some money, them same ones a turn around and wan fight gainst me through me start change me shirt daily: "Them send one gone a obeah man fe try kill me... Want a doctor, want a bush doctor, check up on me structure."'

The year also saw the release of another record that prompted many varied responses, 'Big Belly Man'. By pointing out that 'most of the big belly man them a money man,' the song made a virtue of necessity and made a large gut fashionable for men. The inspiration for the song came from a stage show on which Bailey, Sassafras, and Papa Biggy appeared with Little Twitch. Needless to say, the small, fine-boned Twitch was somewhat overpowered by three of the biggest bellied deejays in Jamaica. The situation prompted Sassafras and Bailey to start urging Twitch to 'get some belly' if he wanted to get popular like them and make some money.

Of all his material, the song that Bailey likes most is 'Chatty Mouth People'. He often wishes he had released it after his big boost so that more people would have heard it, as he feels the message is still important: 'Follow hearsay and you will reach nowhere. That is what is going on. Nuff people is following. The majority of the things that they say they hear, they don't hear it for themselves. Them friend tell them and they just spread it all about.' And once you are at the top, a lot of talk and rumour starts spreading as the top man ends up the target of peoples' envy and jealousy:

It's just envious and them thing there. No wan you to reach nowhere. For instance, for all these years you have been living in the ghetto and moving around and now a little light shine on you, you say, 'Alright I'm going to step up,' and that is the main reason why you are going in a thing. (If you are going in a thing and consider to stay low at all times, is joke!). So, if you start progress now, you live uptown – you no show off nobody – make a little money, change your shirt regular, stop wear tear-up batty pants, they say 'show off, eeee?' They would do it the said way! If you go out and look your own, that's show off according to them.

I don't watch people cause one thing I learned in this business – I feel it's a vital point I'm hitting now – is not everybody going to say you are great. You always find two or three persons going to say 'boy Admiral an idiot.' Critics is a must. One advice me have to give all the youth: go ina it and find you are successful and money start turn is not everyday the people are going to say 'you'. You must come down and a next man come up. There were enough deejay before me, don't it? So in the future you must find a next youth come up. So I must put my own to use so that when my name stop call and I retire, I can look pon my big house and say 'yes, I don't bleech for nothing.' Deejay business is just for a time. You must look to the future.

Me na put all my eggs ina one basket. Me on top now and me have a business a run in Jamaica. Me decide to go in a more business, any business me can see turn money. Because you can't just say you will deejay forever. You must get old or tired or something. So you must put your money to good use, bank it, invest it. Me have the future well planned.

King Kong:
Don't Touch the Gorilla

King Kong

King Kong, the reggae gorilla, began life as Kong Junior (his father, the original King Kong, being Kong Senior). 'He was an old soldier – a big thick man. And through them time there the *King Kong* movie did a gwan them used to call him King Kong. So through me a the only son who him have whe deh ya mongst him the time, they did call me Junior Kong. Now, through me grow with the whole of the youth them and go around, the name just come offa him and eventually step on me.'

Despite public opinion to the contrary, Kong still calls himself 'the ugly one' and insists: 'Yes, I'm really ugly.' He even owns two frighteningly hairy gorilla suits to maintain the image. But although he may lack faith in his looks, he is sure of his singing talents. He just had trouble getting a consistent start going in the business. After a few false starts – like his time as deejay for Family Man's Dread Lion sound system and his first recording, a deejay tune called 'Pink Eye' for Tuff Gong in 1982 – he came to stay in 1985. Kong always meant to be in music. He used to hang around Tuff Gong to watch Bob Marley rehearse with the Wailers, and even after Bob was gone, he still hung around until he made that first record. But his career was interrupted by a prison term. Inside four walls for very close on two years, Kong had time to form a resolve to pursue music seriously. As soon as he came out, he headed for Tubby's and hung around the studio singing and singing and singing until he got his first chance to record. At Tubby's he made 'This Magic Moment', followed by 'Step on My Corn', and then 'Aids', at which point he moved to Jammy's to make 'Trouble Again', 'Legal We Legal', and 'Niceness'.

Kong began his career quite openly with a style he borrowed for the occasion. 'At the time, that style was mashing up the place so anybody that come that way and come good … Me have me own style even up to now. Me versatile. Like if me hear a singer, if me study him, if me just listen him a couple of times, I can sound exactly – or similar – to him. So I made a little thing about me a go step on them corn. But me no want it to sound too much like a throw word thing so me just say – someone step on me corn and me just lick it and it sound a little way and the more me get into it now [the style], the more improve until eventually it's like me rule the style.'

At first, people called Kong an imitator. But he responded by making a song for the accusers called 'Identify Me', in which he sang in every popular voice challenging the listeners to identify which singer he really was. Well, if you hadn't read the label first, it could have fooled you. 'I made that to show them how me versatile. So me just make them know say me sing any style.' 'Identify Me' was actually recorded at Fashion studios when Ossie (Black Solidarity) was in England laying down some rhythms. Kong was voicing a few cuts from his *Identify Me* LP using Fashion rhythms when he heard the 'Identify Me' track and wanted to try it. The song was a popular one, though Kong insists that he does have his own individual style also. 'You hear the song that says "she's on my mind" [on the *Identify Me* LP]? That's my real style. Kinda baby voice. But through me so big and ugly, fe sing in a baby voice … so me just ruff it out.'

Ironically, Horace Ferguson claims that his 'Do Not Touch the General' was written off the song 'Identify Me'. 'When we adapt all other singer type of voice,' Horace reports, 'he copy them and he sound really like them. But my voice is a baby voice so he can't get my kind of voice.'

Kong is planning even more surprises for his fans. 'Further down the line I have some more different style of tune fe come out. Some more ballad, softer stuff, easy going.' Although all of Kong's material is created by him, none of the songs are actually written out. Rather they are inspirations of the moment. 'I get a better inspiration that way. If I sit down and write a song, it's like a headache to me. You see, just sit down and thinking about it, that's me – same way it just come to me. Some people have to write but if I write it give me problem. It's like a headache.'

He also has a special song he thought out while in jail that he wants to record, but he's waiting for the time when he can assemble the right musicians to play the rhythm professionally. 'It's like a Bunny Wailer kinda stuff. You can't just run go do them tune. You have fe really build them and get them organised. This dancehall thing, this is just to give you a break.'

Kong is confident he can make it. 'I know for a fact that I'm going to be a star – a big star. And me na give up. I know the potential whe me have and what me can do. And me a go do it. You only want to have faith and that a whe me have. Cause I've been through the lowest of the lowest and no give up.'

That lowest point was his last stay in prison – G.P. – in the remand block while awaiting the completion of his case. After languishing for one year and eleven months, he was cleared of the charges and set free. 'Three time me go a G.P. Me a bad boy, you know. But you see, when me go a jail, it just like a college. Everything done for a purpose and I feel like it done to me for a purpose to know myself. The way I used to think – me go a jail but me only get wickeder and tougher so me always continue going there cause me always continue doing back the same thing cause it make me get wickeder, make you just say, "ooooo me no care." And when you think now and say, "boy them set this," and if you continue to follow the step and go on the same way for the rest of your life, when you old you are in the same way. So me just check back now and say, "boy me wan live somewhere comfortable."' The only solution was music. 'Me just decide that the only way for me is just take it up more serious.'

'There is always a turning point in life and that for me was a turning point.' It hasn't always been easy in the music business either, but Kong is satisfied that he made the right move. 'Me glad now.'

Beth Lesser
Reggae Quarterly 1, No. 8 (1987)

King Jammy's LP Discography

compiled by Ray Hurford and Andrew Lee
January 2002

Admiral Bailey, *Born Champion*, Live and Love, UK 1989
Admiral Bailey, *Kill Them with It*, Live and Love, UK 1987
Admiral Bailey, *Science Again*, Rohit, US 1990
Admiral Bailey, *Undisputed*, Jammys, JA 1987
Admiral Tibett, *Come into the Light*, Live and Love, UK 1987
Andy, Horace, *Haul and Jack Up*, Live and Love, UK 1987
Anthony, Pad, *Nuff Niceness*, Jammys, JA 1985
Benji, Risto, *Wickedest DJ*, VP, US 1993
Black Crucials, *Mr Sonny*, Jammys, JA 1985
Black Uhuru, *In Dub*, CSA, UK 1982
Black Uhuru, *Love Crisis*, Third World, UK 1977
Black Uhuru, *Black Sounds of Freedom*, Greensleeves, UK 1981
Boothe, Ken, *Call Me*, Rohit, US 1990
Bounty Killer, *Down in the Ghetto*, Greensleeves, UK 1994
Bounty Killer, *Ghetto Grammar*, Greensleeves, UK 1997
Bounty Killer, *Jamaica's Most Wanted*, Greensleeves, UK 1994
Bounty Killer & Beenie Man, *Guns Out*, Greensleeves, UK 1994
Brown, Barry, *Showcase*, Jammys, JA 1980
Brown, Dennis, *Slow Down*, Greensleeves, UK 1985
Brown, Dennis, *The Exit*, Trojan, UK 1986
Brown, Dennis, *Unforgettable*, Jammys, JA 1993
Bushman, *Total Commitment*, Greensleeves, UK 1999
Campbell, Al, *Ain't too Proud to Beg*, Live and Love, UK 1990
Chaka Demus, *Bad Bad Chaka*, Jammys, JA 1994
Chaka Demus & Shabba Ranks, *Rough and Rugged*, Live and Love, UK 1990
Clarke, Johnny, *Think About It*, Super Power, UK 1988
Cobra, *Mr. Pleasure*, VP, US 1993
Cobra, *Venom*, Greensleeves, UK 1993
Cocoa Tea, *Come Again*, Live and Love, UK 1987
Cocoa Tea, *I Am the Toughest*, Jammys, JA 1992
Cocoa Tea, *The Marshall*, Jammys, JA 1986
Courtney Melody, *Bad Boy Reggae*, Jammys, JA 1990
Cultural Roots, *Running Back to Me*, Mango, UK 1988
Delgado, Junior, *Moving Down the Line*, Live and Love, US 1986
Delgado, Junior, *Roadblock*, Blue Mountain, UK 1987
Dominick, *Ready for Dominick*, Mango, UK 1988
Fraser, Dean, *Big Bad Sax*, Super Power, UK 1988
Galaxy P, *Old Friends*, Charm, UK 1993
Gibbons, Leroy, *Four Season Lover*, Super Power, UK 1988
Half Pint, *Money Man Skank*, Jammys, JA 1984
Half Pint, *Pick Your Choice*, VP, US 1993
Half Pint, *One in a Million*, Greensleeves, UK 1984
Home T, *No Time to Waste*, Jammys, JA
Isaacs, Gregory, *Come Along*, Live and Love, UK 1988
Isaacs, Gregory, *Let's Go Dancing*, Rohit, US 1989
Isaacs, Gregory, *Two Time Loser*, Jammys, JA 1995
Isaacs, Gregory, *Who's Gonna Take You Home*, Rohit, US 1990
Johnny P, *Reggae Dancehall Sensation*, Rohit, US 1970

Johnson, Anthony, *A Yah We Deh*, Jammys, JA 1985
King Kong, *Trouble Again*, Greensleeves, UK 1986
Little John, *Clarkes Booty*, Live and Love, US 1986
Lt. Stitchie, *Great Ambition*, Super Power, UK 1987
Lt. Stitchie, *Ghetto Soldier*, Greensleeves, UK 1994
Major Worries, *Babylon Boops*, Jammys, JA 1986
Minott, Echo, *What the Hell*, Jammys, JA 1987
Minott, Sugar, *Bitter Sweet*, Warrior, UK 1979
Minott, Sugar, *Touch of Class*, Jammys, JA 1990
Morgan Heritage, *One Calling*, Greensleeves, UK 1997
Mundell, Hugh & Lacksley Castell, *Jah Fire*, Live and Love, UK 1980
Murvin, Junior, *Apartheid*, Greensleeves, UK 1986
Nicodemus, *Dancehall Style*, Black Joy, UK 1982
Nicodemus, *Old Veteran*, VP, US 1992
Ninjaman, *Hollow Point Bad Boy*, Greensleeves, UK 1994
Ninjaman, *Warning You Now*, Jammys 1991
Nitty Gritty, *Turbo Charged*, Greensleeves, UK 1986
Nitty Gritty & King Kong, *Musical Confrontation*, Jammys, JA 1986
Osbourne, Johnny, *Fally Ranking*, Positive Sounds, UK 1980
Osbourne, Johnny, *Musical Chopper*, Jammys, JA 1983
Osbourne, Johnny, *Rub a Dub Soldier*, Jammys, JA 1985
Osbourne, Johnny, *Water Pumping*, Greensleeves, UK 1983
Palmer, Michael, *I'm So Attractive*, Jammys, JA 1985
Panhead, *Punny Printer*, Jammys, JA
Paul, Frankie, *Casanova*, Live and Love, UK 1988
Paul, Frankie, *Close to You*, Jammys, JA 1991
Paul, Frankie, *Heartical Don*, Super Power, JA 1990
Paul, Frankie, *Live and Love*, Jammys, JA
Paul, Frankie, *Money Talk*, Jammys, JA
Paul, Frankie, *Sara*, Live and Love, UK 1987
Paul, Frankie, *Still Alive*, Jammys, JA 1986
Paul, Frankie, *Tomorrow*, Dynamic
Paul, Frankie & Micheal Palmer, *Double Trouble*, Greensleeves, UK 1984
Peck, Gregory, *Lyrics Factory*, Jammys, JA
Penny Irie, *Hotness*, VP, US 1992
Phillips, Noel, *Youthman Vibration*, Jammys, JA 1981
Pinchers, *Agony*, Jammys, JA 1987
Pinchers, *Bandelero*, Jammys, JA 1991
Pinchers, *Got to Be Me*, Live and Love, UK 1987
Prince Jammy, *Dub War Vol 1*, Vista Sounds, UK 1985
Prince Jammy, *In Lion Dub Style*, Third World, UK 1977
Prince Jammy, *Jammys vs Tubbys*, Sky Juice, UK 1983
Prince Jammy, *Kamikazi Dub*, Trojan, UK 1979
Prince Jammys, *Osbourne in Dub*, CSA, UK 1983
Prince Jammy, *Prince Jammys Destroys the Invaders*, Greensleeves, UK 1982
Prince Jammy, *Strictly Dub*, Jammys, JA 1981
Prince Jammy vs Crucial Bunny, *Fatman Dub*, Contest Star, UK 1980
Prince Jammy vs Scientist, *Big Showdown*, Greensleeves, UK 1980

Prince Jammy vs Scientist, *Jammy & Scientist Strike Back*, Trojan, UK 1982
Prince Jammy & Wayne Smith, *Sleng Teng and Computerized Dub*, Greensleeves, UK 1992
Reid, Junior, *Boom Shack A Lack*, Greensleeves, UK 1985
Shabba Ranks, *Love Punanny Bad*, Jammys, JA 1993
Shabba Ranks, *Star of the '90s*, Jammys, JA 1990
Shabba Ranks & Chaka Demus, *Rough and Rugged*, Super Power, UK 1989
Silk, Garnett, *Silky Mood*, VP, US 1995
Smart, Leroy, *We Rule Everytime*, Jammys, JA 1985
Smith, Wayne, *Sleng Teng*, Greensleeves, UK 1986
Smith, Wayne, *Super Smoker*, Chartbound, UK 1985
Smith, Wayne, *Youthman Skanking*, Black Joy, UK 1982
Sparks, Trevor, *Cool Out*, Live and Love, UK 1988
Stephens, Richie, *Sincerely Jammys*, JA
Stewart, Tinga, *No Drugs*, Live and Love, UK 1988
Super Black, *We Ready fe Them*, Live and Love, US 1987
Thriller U, *The Danger*, Jammys, JA 1989
Thriller U, *Waiting for You*, Live and Love, UK 1989
Tiger, *Love Affair*, Rohit, US
Tiger, *Shocking Colour*, Jammys, JA 1989
Tiger, *Reggae Dancehall Sensation*, Rohit, US 1981
Tonto Irie, *Jammys Posse*, Jammys, JA 1990
Travellers, *Black Black Minds*, Third World, UK 1977
Tuffest, *Reggae Dancehall Sensation*, Rohit, US
Turner, Chuck, *One the Hard Way*, Live and Love, UK 1988
U Black, *Westbound Thing a Swing*, Third World, UK 1977
V/A, *16 Reggae Hits*, Live and Love, UK 1989
V/A, *Bellyas*, Greensleeves, UK 2000
V/A, *Carolina My Darling*, VP, US 1993
V/A, *Cradle Robber*, Super Power
V/A, *Crowning of Prince Jammy*, Pressure Sounds, UK 1999
V/A, *DJ Confrontation*, Live and Love, UK 1987
V/A, *DJ's Choice*, VP, US 2000
V/A, *DJ's Greatest*, Live and Love, UK 1988
V/A, *DJ's Greatest Vol 2*, Live and Love, UK 1988
V/A, *Double Twin Spin Vol 1*, Live and Love, UK 1987
V/A, *Dub Plates Vol 1*, Jammys, JA
V/A, *Duck Dance Competition*, Jammys, JA 1988
V/A, *Echoes vs Rockers FM*, Super Power, UK 1987
V/A, *Five the Hard Way*, Live and Love, US 1986
V/A, *Four the Hard Way*, Jammys JA
V/A, *Further East*, Live and Love, UK 1990
V/A, *Further East Vol 2*, Live and Love
V/A, *Ghetto Vibes/Answer Excursion*, VP, US 1993
V/A, *Gilbert is a Disaster*, Live and Love, UK 1988
V/A, *Jam Session Vol 1*, Live and Love, UK 1988
V/A, *Jammys Chartbusters*, Jammys, JA 1989
V/A, *Killer Style Dub*, Jammys JA
V/A, *King Jammys Angels*, Live and Love, UK 1988

V/A, *King Jammys Presents Vol 1*, Jammys, JA
V/A, *King Jammys Presents Vol 4*, Live and Love
V/A, *King Jammys Presents Vol 5*, Live and Love
V/A, *Kings of Dancehall Vol 2*, Artists Only
V/A, *Mad Them Wid It/Carolina*, Jammys, JA
V/A, *Magician*, Jammys, JA
V/A, *Mix Up and Blend*, Live and Love
V/A, *Prince Jammys Presents Vol 2*, Jammys, JA 1986
V/A, *Prince Jammys Presents Vol 3*, Live and Love, UK 1987
V/A, *Prince Jammys Presents Vol 4*, Live and Love, UK 1987
V/A, *Reggae Hits Forever Vol 1*, Super Power, UK
V/A, *Riddim Rulers*, Jammys, JA
V/A, *Righteousness*, Jammys, JA
V/A, *Roots Reality*, Mention
V/A, *Sleng Teng*, Jammys, JA 1985
V/A, *Sleng Teng Extravaganza Vol 2*, Jammys, JA 1985
V/A, *Sleng Teng Extravanganza 95*, Greensleeves, UK 1995
V/A, *Sound Clash Sound 1*, Super Power, UK 1989
V/A, *Sound Clash Sound 2*, Super Power, UK 1989
V/A, *Stalag 17*, Jammys, JA 1985
V/A, *Star Studded General*, VP, US 1993.
V/A, *Strictly Dancehall Vibes Vol 1*, Jammys, JA
V/A, *Super Power Vol 1*, Super Power
V/A, *Super Power Vol 2*, Super Power
V/A, *Superpower Presents Whip*, Super Power
V/A, *Superstar Hit Parade*, Greensleeves, UK 1986
V/A, *Superstar Hit Parade Vol 2*, Live and Love, US 1986
V/A, *Superstar Hit Parade Vol 3*, Live and Love, UK 1987
V/A, *Superstar Hit Parade Vol 4*, Live and Love, UK 1988
V/A, *Superstar Hit Parade Vol 5*, Live and Love
V/A, *Superstar Hit Parade Vol 6*, Live and Love
V/A, *Superstar Hit Parade Vol 7*, Live and Love
V/A, *Ten To One*, Jammys, JA 1985
V/A, *Top 10 '89 Compilation*, Super Power, UK 1989
V/A, *Top Ten Vol 3*, Super Power
V/A, *Total Recall 5*, VP
V/A, *Whip*, Imaj
V/A, *Wicked Everywhere*, Super Power
V/A, *No Ice Cream Style*, VP
V/A, *A Man and His Music Computer Style*, Jammys
V/A, *A Man and His Music Hits Style*, Jammys
V/A, *Memories Unforgettable Experience*, Live And Love
Wailing Souls, *Stormy Night*, Rohit, US
Wales, Josey, *Cowboy Style*, Greensleeves, UK 1993
Wales, Josey, *Ha Fe Say So*, Jammys, JA 1987
Wales, Josey, *Nuh Lef Jamaica*, Mango, UK 1988
Wales, Josey, *Special Prayer*, Jammys, JA 1989